Preparation Guide for the RHIA and RHIT Examinations
2nd Edition

Ruth Leroy, MHS, RHIA

PRG Publishing, Inc.
Professional Review Guides, Inc.

Preparation Guide for the RHIA and RHIT Examinations, 2nd Edition, by Ruth Leroy

Published by: **PRG Publishing, Inc.**
Professional Review Guides
P. O. Box 528
St. Petersburg, Florida 33731
Phone: (727) 526-3163
FAX: (727) 526-4474
Toll Free: (888) 383-PRG1~or~(888) 383-7741
E-mail: pjsprg@aol.com

ISBN: 1-932152-14-8
Printed in the United States of America

Contributing authors:
Lee Thomas. MHS, RHIA, Assistant Professor, Program Director, Chicago State University
Barbara Price, MPA, RHIA, Assistant Professor, Health Information Administration Program, Chicago State University

Editor: Patricia Schnering, RHIA, CCS

Disclaimer of Warranty

It is the authors' sincerest hope that each student using this preparation guide will pass the national examination. The authors suggest that students avail themselves of all resources possible including text books, class notes and materials obtained during their educational process, attendance at examination review sessions, participation in study groups and the use of other examination review books.

for the students.....

Introduction

The intent of this guide is to provide an organizational framework for preparing for the RHIA and RHIT certification examination. The format is designed to focus attention on the intent of the exam, which is to measure one's knowledge and competence in the current health information profession. This guide is not meant to be a quick fix to replace a proper study program. It is designed to be used as a tool to structure, assist and enhance the study and test preparation activities.

About the Authors

Ruth A. Leroy, MHS, RHIA

Ruth Leroy is a 1971 graduate of Northern Michigan University with a BA in Education. After ten years of teaching in the Chicago Public Schools, she decided to pursue a change in career. This was accomplished when she received her degree in Health Information Management from Chicago State University in 1982. Ms. Leroy received her Master's degree in Health Science Education from Governors State University in 1989. Her experience has included time as an Assistant Director at a multi-level hospital, Quality Assurance Coordinator with an HMO and as a Director of Medical Records, Out-Patient Services and Risk Management at a rehabilitation hospital. For the past fourteen years, she has been on the faculty at Chicago State University as an Assistant Professor in the HIM Program. In June of 1996, Professor Leroy was presented with the Faculty Excellence Award for Outstanding Achievement in teaching, research, creative activity and service.

Contributing Authors

Leona Thomas, MHS, RHIA

Leona Thomas is a graduate of the University of Colorado's Medical Record Administration Program. She also has a Master's degree in Health Science from Governors State University. Her past work experience is varied. Prior to her present position, she acted as editor at the AHIMA. For the last 20 years, she has been on the faculty as an Assistant Professor at Chicago State University. For the past 10 years, she has served as Program Director of the Health Information Administration Program at Chicago State University.

Barbara Price, MPA, RHIA

Barbara Price is a graduate of the Health Information Management program at Chicago State University. She received her Master of Public Administration degree from the University of Illinois at Chicago. She is a Member of the National Honor Society for Public Affairs and Administration. She is currently pursuing a doctorate in Instructional Technology at Northern Illinois University, DeKalb, Illinois. Prior to her current position, she was Director of Health Information Services and Clinical Assessment at Advocate Healthcare-Trinity Hospital. Her responsibilities included leadership of the Health Information Services, Quality Improvement, Admitting, Medical Staff and Library Services departments. Ms. Price has also held positions as Director and Assistant Director of Health Information Management Departments. She is currently an Assistant Professor in the Health Information Administration at Chicago State University. In 1999, Professor Price was awarded the honor of Excellence in Teaching.

Table of Contents

SECTION 3   *Content Outlines (continued)*

SECTION 4   *Study Tools*

INDEX

ABOUT THE DOMAINS

Roles and Functions Study

One of the most important aspects of your study preparation is to gain an in-depth understanding of the registration exam specifications known as the domains, subdomains and competency statements/test specifications. How can this be accomplished? To put it another way, how can you, as a graduate of an accredited Health Information Program, best prepare for the certification exam? The answer to this question lies with the American Health Information Management Association's (AHIMA) Council on Certification (COC). It is the COC's responsibility to discern which job tasks are most frequently performed by newly certified practitioners. Following that course, the COC identifies which job tasks are critical to entry level practice. The process of identifying those critical job functions is accomplished by conducting a job analysis. The job analysis is achieved by performing a research study. This research study is known as the Roles and Functions Study. The Roles and Functions Study is sponsored by the AHIMA but the study itself is conducted by an outside research team.

The process begins with the COC contracting for a job analysis research study. The study is performed on a significant portion of recently certified RHIAs and RHITs. The COC's objective is to determine how entry level practice is evolving for both the RHIA and RHIT and to revise the domains, subdomains and test specifications accordingly. Of equal importance is that the Roles and Functions Study validates the certifying examination as relevant and applicable.

The entry level tasks for RHIAs and RHITs are grouped into five domains:
- Healthcare Data
- Health Information Analysis
- Healthcare Environment
- Information Technology and Systems
- Organization and Management

The five domains are further divided into subdomains. Each of the subdomains is modified by task statements. These five domains and their subdomains are the same for the RHIA and RHIT, although the task statements frequently differ.

Weights are assigned for each domain and subdomain; however, weights are not assigned for the task statements. The weights are assigned as an indicator of the emphasis and importance that is given to a particular domain or subdomain as it relates to the health information practice.

On the following page, **Table 1** displays the domains and subdomains and their assigned weights. This table shows a comparison of the weights, revealing how the weights can differ substantially between the RHIA and the RHIT. As an example, four times as much emphasis is placed in the area of organization and management for the RHIA, while much greater importance is given to healthcare data and information for the RHIT.

TABLE 1

Domains and Subdomains and equivalent weights for the RHIA and RHIT Certification Exams

DOMAIN	DOMAIN SUBDOMAIN	RHIA QUESTIONS/WEIGHTS		RHIT QUESTIONS/WEIGHTS	
I	**Healthcare Data**	**40**	**25%**	**53**	**41%**
	Subdomain				
	A. Data Structure, Content & Use	24	15%	27	20%
	B. Clinical Classification Systems ICD-9-CM Coding	8	5%	13	10%
	C Clinical Classification Systems-CPT-4 Coding	8	5%	13	10%
II	**Health Information Analysis**	**24**	**15%**	**21****	**16%**
	Subdomain				
	A. Healthcare Statistics & Research	15	10%		
	B. Clinical Quality Assessment and Performance Improvement	9	5%		
III	**Health Care Environment**	**32**	**20%**	**26**	**20%**
	Subdomain				
	A. Healthcare Delivery Systems	8	5%	8	6-7%
	B. Legal and Ethical Issues	12	7.5%	8	6-7%
	C. Healthcare Information Requirements and Standards	12	7.5%	10	7-8%
IV	**Information Technology and Systems**	**24**	**15%**	**16**	**12%**
	Subdomain				
	A. Information Technology	12	7.5%	8	6-7%
	B. Health Information Systems	12	7.5%	8	6-7%
V	**RHIA: Organization and Management**	**40**	**25%**		
	Subdomain				
	A. Human Resource Management	20	12.5%		
	B. Health Information Services Management	20	12.5%		
	RHIT: **Organization and Supervision**			**14****	**11%**
TOTAL		**160***	**100%**	**130***	**100%**

*The RHIT exam is a 3.5 hour, 150-item examination consisting of 130 scored items and 20 pretest items.

The RHIA exam is a 4 hour, 180-item examination consisting of 160 scored items and 20 pretest items.

**No subdomains accompany this domain, only task statements.

(Note: This breakdown is accurate as of the 2003 certification exam. This analysis is subject to change. Look to AHIMA's web page for the most current information regarding the exam blueprint.)

Cognitive Levels

In addition to a weight assigned to each of the domains and subdomains, cognitive levels are also assigned. Cognitive levels were not established for the task statements. The cognitive levels that are used for the test questions on the certification exam are: recall (or knowledge), application and analysis. Each cognitive level relates to a corresponding ability to think and reason. For example, a knowledge question requires the lowest level of thinking. When answering a recall (knowledge) question, one simply needs to remember the needed information. On the other hand, an analysis question requires the highest level of thinking. To respond to an analysis question, one is required to recall the information and compare, contrast and/or evaluate the information needed. **Table 2** provides a description of the three cognitive levels. A more detailed discussion, along with examples of these cognitive levels, is given in Section 2 of this guide. **Table 3** illustrates the relationship of the cognitive levels to the subdomains. Once again, a comparison is made between the RHIA's and the RHIT's cognitive ranges.

TABLE 2 Comparisons of Cognitive Levels

COGNITIVE LEVEL	PURPOSE	WHAT IS REQUIRED
RECALL **or** **KNOWLEDGE**	Remembering previously learned material	Information recalled ranges from specific facts (i.e. a physiatrist specializes in what type of medicine) to complex formulae such as those used in the Medicare Program for DRG payment. Verbs used in course objectives at the knowledge/recall level include: define, describe, identify, label, list, match, state, select etc.
APPLICATION	Ability to use new and learned information in a new and concrete situation	This cognitive level requires the application of: rules, methods, concepts, principles, laws and theories. Verbs used in course objectives at the application level are: changes, computes, demonstrates, discovers, modifies, operates, predicts, prepares, produces, shows, solves, uses etc.
ANALYSIS	Ability to know, understand and apply new information appropriately by interpreting data and recognizing the interrelationships; breaking information into its component parts so that its organizational structure may be understood	Information that is analyzed includes: identification of parts, analysis of the relationship between the parts and recognition of the organizational principle involved. Analysis requires an understanding of both the content and structural form of the material. Verbs used in course objectives at the analysis level are: break down, diagram, differentiate, illustrate, infer, relate, select and separate.

TABLE 3

Relationship of subdomains to cognitive levels and percentage of test questions at each level

DOMAIN	DOMAIN SUBDOMAIN	RHIA COGNITIVE LEVELS			RHIT COGNITIVE LEVELS		
		Total Questions-40			Total Questions-53		
I	**Healthcare Data** Subdomain	RE	AP	AN	RE	AP	AN
	A. Data Structure, Content & Use	12%	12%	35%	11%	9%	30%
	B. Clinical Classification System ICD-9-CM Coding	8%	12%		10%	15%	
	C. Clinical Classifications System CPT Coding	8%	12%		10%	15%	
		Total Questions-24			Total Questions-21		
II	**Health Information Analysis** Subdomain						
	A. Healthcare Statistics and Research	13%	38%	13%	19%	61%	21%
	B. Clinical Quality Assessment and Performance Improvement	8%	8%	20%	N/A	N/A	N/A
		Total Questions-32			Total Questions-26		
III	**Health Care Environment** Subdomain						
	A. Healthcare Delivery Systems	9%	16%	0%	12%	19%	0%
	B. Legal and Ethical Issues	9%	19%	9%	12%	19%	0%
	C. Healthcare Information Requirements and Standards	6%	9%	22%	12%	19%	7%
		Total Questions-24			Total Questions-16		
IV	**Information Technology and Systems** Subdomain						
	A. Information Technology	8%	29%	13%	19%	31%	0%
	B. Health Information Systems	8%	29%	13%	19%	31%	0%
		Total Questions-40			Total Questions-14		
V	**RHIA-Organization and Management** Subdomain						
	A. Human Resource Management	10%	30%	10%			
	B. Health Information Services Management	10%	10%	30%			
	RHIT- Organization and Supervision				21%	57%	21%
TOTAL questions		160			130		
TOTAL questions per cognitive level		37	70	53	38	67	25
TOTAL percentage per cognitive level		23%	44%	33%	29%	52%	19%

(Note: This breakdown is accurate as of the 2003 certification exam. This analysis is subject to change. Look to AHIMA's web page for the most current information regarding the exam blueprint.)

Cross Indexes

On the following pages, you will find cross indexes for the RHIA and RHIT domains. The first set of cross-indexes presents each competency statement, per domain and subdomain, and associates that competency statement with a specific health information content area. The cross index can help with study preparation by providing additional interpretation for the task statements by associating a content area with them. It is not surprising that specific content areas have not been directly linked to a task statement. The profile of the HIM professional is merging with new healthcare roles, making it more difficult to simply associate a job task to a particular content area. But, since it may be easier to direct your study efforts in a content oriented fashion, the cross-index is provided.

In the event that you would like to approach your study with a focus on the subdomains, a second set of indexes is included. The second set associates the health information content to specific subdomains. No matter what approach you take to integrate the subdomains into your studying, the cross-indexes can ease that transition.

All of this information points in one direction. You will need to know and understand the task competency statements. Incorporating the task statements into your study efforts should be an integral part of your exam preparations. All your study planning should be directed to include them. Remember, the task statements reflect what you are expected to assimilate and master, not only for the registration exam, but for your entry level role as a HIM professional.

Note: *The author determined the assignment of a competency to content area. The AHIMA has not provided an official cross index.*

RHIA

CROSS INDEX: Task Competencies to Health Information Content Area

I. DOMAIN: HEALTH CARE DATA		

TASK	Task/Competency Statement	Content Area
A. Subdomain: Data Structure, Content and Use		
1.	Verify timeliness, completeness, accuracy and appropriateness of data and data sources (e.g., patient care, management, billing reports and/or databases).	Health Records Classification Systems
2.	Conduct qualitative analysis to assure that documentation in the health record supports the diagnosis and reflects the progress, clinical findings and discharge status.	Health Records Quality Assessment Classification Systems Medical Science
3.	Assist in the facility's billing process.	Information Systems Classification Systems
4.	Validate coding accuracy using clinical information found in the health record.	Classification Systems Medical Science Quality Assessment
B. Subdomain: Clinical Classification Systems ICD-9-CM Coding		
1.	Assign diagnosis/procedure codes using ICD-9-CM.	Coding/Classification Systems
C. Subdomain: Clinical Classification Systems CPT Coding		
1.	Assign diagnosis/procedure codes using CPT/HCPCS.	Coding/Classification Systems
II. DOMAIN: HEALTH INFORMATION ANALYSIS		
A. Subdomain: Healthcare Statistics and Research		
1.	Abstract records for department indices/databases/registries.	Health Records Information Systems
2.	Collect data for quality management, utilization management, risk management and other patient care related studies.	Quality Assessment Health Records
3.	Calculate and interpret healthcare statistics.	Statistics Quality Assessment
4.	Present data in verbal and written forms.	Statistics Quality Assessment
B. Subdomain: Clinical Quality Assessment and Performance Improvement		
1.	Participate in facility-wide quality management program.	Quality Assessment
2.	Analyze clinical data to identify trends.	Statistics Quality Assessment

III. DOMAIN: HEALTHCARE ENVIRONMENT

A. Subdomain: Healthcare Delivery Systems

1.	Interpret and apply laws, accreditation, licensure and certification standards, monitor changes and communicate information-related changes to others in the facility.	All content areas with attention paid to legal and record retention
2.	Understand the role of various providers and disciplines throughout the continuum of healthcare services.	All content areas with attention paid to legal and record retention

B. Subdomain: Legal and Ethical Issues

1.	Release patient-specific data to authorized users.	Legal
2.	Request patient-specific information from other sources.	Legal
3.	Summarize patient encounter data for release to authorized users.	Legal
4.	Develop policies and procedures to protect unauthorized access to patient records.	Legal/Management
5.	Assist in developing facility-wide confidentiality policies.	Legal/Management

C. Subdomain: Healthcare Information Requirements and Standards

1.	Assist in developing health record documentation guidelines.	Health Records Management
2.	Perform quantitative analysis of health records to evaluate compliance with regulations and standards.	Health Records Quality Assessment
3.	Perform qualitative analysis of health records to evaluate compliance.	Health Records Quality Assessment Management
4.	Assist in preparing the facility of an accreditation, licensing and/or certification survey.	All
5.	Develop and demonstrate HIM service compliance with relevant regulations and accreditation standards.	All
6.	Ensure facility-wide adherence to health information services' compliance with regulatory requirements (e.g., ICD-9-CM cooperating parties coding guidelines, CMS Compliance Plan, Correct Coding Initiative).	All

IV. DOMAIN: INFORMATION TECHNOLOGY AND SYSTEMS

A. Subdomain: Information Technology and Systems

1.	Use common software packages (e.g., spreadsheets, databases, word processing, graphics, presentation, statistical, e-mail).	Information Systems All
2.	Use electronic or imaging technology to store medical records.	Retention & Retrieval
3.	Query facility-wide databases to retrieve information.	Information Systems Retention & Retrieval Quality Assessment
4.	Generate reports from various databases.	Information Systems Quality Assessment
5.	Protect data integrity and validity using software or hardware technology.	Information Systems
6.	Enforce confidentiality and security measures to protect electronic information.	Information Systems Legal
7.	Identify common software problems.	Information Systems
8.	Design data quality controls and edits.	Information Systems
9.	Participate in development of strategic and operational plans for facility-wide information systems.	Information Systems Management

B. Subdomain: Health Information Systems

1.	Collect and report data on incomplete records and timeliness of record completion.	Health Records Management
2.	Maintain filing and retrieval systems for paper-based patient records.	Retention & Retrieval
3.	Maintain integrity of master patient/client index.	Retention & Retrieval
4.	Maintain integrity of patient numbering and filing systems.	Retention & Retrieval
5.	Design forms, computer input screens and other health record documentation tools.	Health Records
6.	Evaluate software packages to determine that they meet user needs.	Information Systems Management

V. DOMAIN: ORGANIZATION AND MANAGEMENT

A. Subdomain: Human Resources Management

1.	Interview prospective employees.	Human Resource Management
2.	Hire new employees.	Human Resource Management
3.	Develop and implement new staff orientation and training programs.	Human Resource Management
4.	Supervise staff.	Management
5.	Collect data on employee performance.	Management
6.	Conduct performance appraisals.	Human Resource Management

7.	Counsel, discipline and terminate staff.	Human Resource Management
8.	Perform job analyses.	Human Resource Management
9.	Develop job descriptions.	Human Resource Management
10.	Conduct in-service education programs on topics related to health information services.	Human Resource Management
11.	Develop and support work teams.	Management
B. Subdomain: Health Information Services Management		
1.	Monitor staffing levels, turnaround time, productivity and workflow.	Financial Management
2.	Assign projects and tasks to appropriate staff.	Management
3.	Develop productivity and control measures.	Financial Management
4.	Benchmark staff performance data in relation to department/facility performance standards.	Financial Management
5.	Determine resources (equipment and supplies) to meet workload needs.	Financial Management
6.	Develop departmental policies and procedures.	Management
7.	Develop strategic plans, goals and objectives for area of responsibility and communicate to staff.	Management
8.	Participate in intra-departmental teams/committees.	Management
9.	Participate in facility-wide teams/committees responsible for health information services issues.	Management
10.	Coordinate inter-departmental and/or intra-departmental services.	Management
11.	Provide consultation, education and training to users of health information services.	Management
12.	Prepare budgets with accompanying justification and monitor adherence.	Financial Management
13.	Evaluate effectiveness of department operations and services.	Management
14.	Develop quality control/improvement systems for departmental processes and use quality improvement tools and techniques to improve processes.	Management Quality Assessment
15.	Manage special projects.	Management
16.	Plan and conduct meetings.	Management
17.	Resolve customer complaints.	Management
18.	Identify departmental resource requirements, determine cost/benefits, communicate requirements to vendors and evaluate vendor proposals.	Financial Management
19.	Assist in redesigning/re-engineering departmental services and operations.	Management
20.	Prioritize department functions and services.	Management

BLUEPRINT OF THE RHIA REGISTRATION EXAM

There are 71 task/competency statements for the RHIA. As stated previously in this guide, the certification exam questions are based on these statements. The chart and table below are graphic visualizations of the percentages and number of exam questions that correlate to each of the subdomains. This will give a better understanding of the emphasis placed on a subdomain in relation to an exam question. This way, study endeavors can be planned accordingly.

Percentage of Exam Questions Per Domain

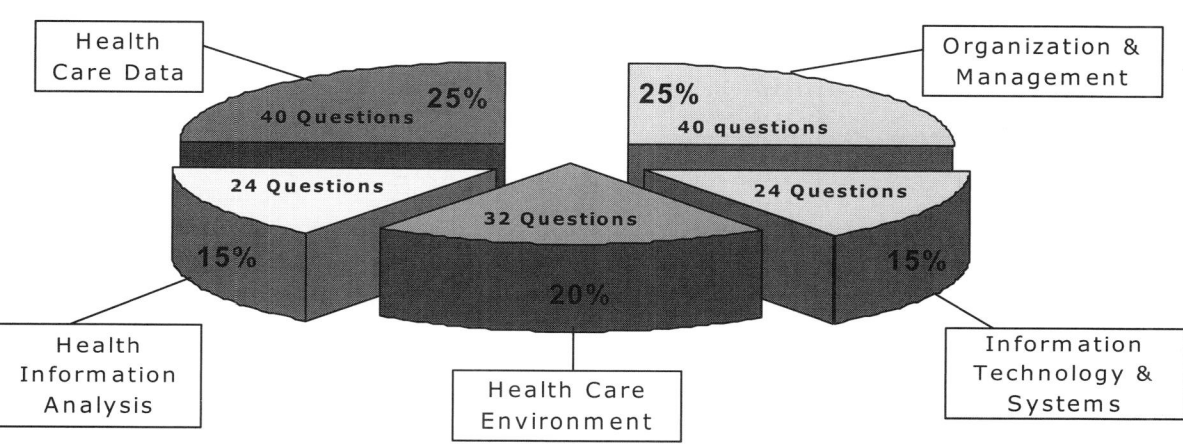

Number of Questions Per Subdomain: RHIA Examination	
Data Structure, Content and Use	24
Clinical Classification Systems ICD-9-CM	8
Clinical Classification Systems CPT/HCPCS	8
Health Care Statistics and Research	15
Clinical Quality Assessment and Performance Improvement	9
Health Care Delivery Systems	8
Legal and Ethical Issues	12
Information Requirements and Standards	12
Information Technology	12
Health Information Systems	12
Human Resource Management	20
Health Information Services Management	20

Please note: This breakdown of questions to subdomains does not include the additional 20 questions that are not scored.

CROSS INDEX: HEALTH INFORMATION CONTENT AREA TO TASK COMPETENCIES

General Content Areas	Domain, Subdomain and Task Competency
Health Records	I.A.1, I.A.2
	II.A.1, II.A.2
	III.A.1, III.A.2, III.C.1, III.C.2, III.C.3, III.C.4, III.C.5, III.C.6
	IV.A.1, IV.B.1, IV.B.5
Information Retention and Retrieval	III.A.1, III.A.2, III.C.4, III.C.5, III.C.6
	IV.A.1, IV.A.2, IV.B.2, IV.B.3, IV.B.4
Classification and Indexing Systems	I.A.1, I.A.2, I.A.3, I.A.4, I.B.1
	III.A.1, III.A.2, III.C.4, III.C.5, III.C.6
	IV.A.1
Coding	I.B.1, I.B.2
	III.A.1, III.A.2, III.C.4, III.C.5, III.C.6
	IV.A.1
Medical Sciences	I.A.2, I.A.4
	III.A.1, III.A.2, III.C.4, III.C.5, III.C.6
Statistics and Research	II.A.3, II.A.4, II.B.2
	III.A.1, III.A.2, III.C.4, III.C.5, III.C.6
	IV.A.1
Quality Assessment and Improvement	I.A.2, I.A.4
	II.A.2, II.A.3, II.A.4, II.B.1, II.B.2
	III.A.1, III.A.2, III.C.2, III.C.3, III.C.4, III.C.5, III.C.6
	IV.A.1, IV.A.3
Health Law	III.A.1, III.A.2, III.B.1, III.B.2, III.B.3, III.B.4, III.B.5, III.C.4, III.C.5, III.C.6
	IV.A.1, IV.A.6
Information Systems	I.A.3
	II.B.1
	III.A.1, III.A.2, III.C.4, III.C.5, III.C.6
	IV.A.1, IV.A.3, IV.A.4, IV.A.5, IV.A.6, IV.A.7, IV.A.8, IV.A.9, IV.A.10, IV.B.6
Management	III.A.1, III.A.2, III.B.4, III.B.5, III.C.1, III.C.2, III.C.3, III.C.4, III.C.5, III.C.6
	IV.A.1, IV.A.9, IV.B.1, IV.B.6
	V.A.1, V.A.2, V.A.3, V.A.4, V.A.5, V.A.6, V.A.7, V.A.8, V.A.9, V.A.10, V.A.11, V.B.2, V.B.7, V.B.8, V.B.9, V.B.10, V.B.11, V.B.13, V.B.14, V.B.16, V.B.17, V.B.18, V.B.19, V.B.20
Human Resources	III.A.1, III.A.2, III.C.4, III.C.5, III.C.6
	V.A.1, V.A.2, V.A.3, V.A.6, V.A.7, V.A.8, V.A.9, V.A.10
Financial Management	III.A.1, III.A.2, III.C.4, III.C.5, III.C.6
	V.A.3, V.A.4, V.A.12, V.A.18, V.B.1

RHIT

CROSS INDEX: Task Competencies to Health Information Content Area

TASK	Task/Competency Statement	Content Area
I. DOMAIN: HEALTH CARE DATA		
A. Subdomain: Data Structure, Content and Use		
1.	Verify timeliness, completeness, accuracy and appropriateness of data and data sources (e.g., patient care, management, billing reports and/or databases).	Health Records Classification Systems
2.	Conduct qualitative analysis to assure that documentation in the health record supports the diagnosis and reflects the progress, clinical findings and discharge status.	Health Records Quality Assessment Classification Systems Medical Science
3.	Assist in the facility's billing process.	Information Systems Classification Systems
4.	Validate coding accuracy using clinical information found in the health record.	Classification Systems Medical Science Quality Assessment
B. Subdomain: Clinical Classification Systems ICD-9-CM Coding		
1.	Assign diagnosis/procedure codes using ICD-9-CM.	Coding/Classification Systems
C. Subdomain: Clinical Classification Systems CPT Coding		
1.	Assign diagnosis/procedure codes using CPT/HCPCS.	Coding/Classification Systems
II DOMAIN: HEALTH INFORMATION ANALYSIS		
A. Subdomain: Healthcare Statistics and Research		
1.	Abstract records for department indices, databases and/or registries.	Health Records Information Systems
2.	Collect data for quality management, utilization management, risk management and other patient care related studies.	Quality Assessment Health Records
3.	Participate in facility-wide quality management program.	Quality Assessment
4.	Calculate and interpret healthcare statistics.	Statistics Quality Assessment
5.	Present data in verbal and written forms.	Statistics Quality Assessment

III. DOMAIN: HEALTHCARE ENVIRONMENT

A. Subdomain: Healthcare Delivery Systems

1.	Interpret and apply laws, accreditation, licensure and certification standards, monitor changes and communicate information-related changes to others in the facility.	All content areas with attention paid to legal and record retention
2.	Understand the role of various providers and disciplines throughout the continuum of healthcare services.	All content areas with attention paid to legal and record retention

B. Subdomain: Legal Issues

1.	Release patient-specific data to authorized users.	Legal
2.	Request patient-specific information from other sources.	
3.	Summarize patient encounter data for release to authorized users.	Legal
4.	Maintain and enforce patient health record confidentiality requirements.	Legal

C. Subdomain: Healthcare Information Requirements and Standards

1.	Assist in developing health record documentation guidelines.	Health Records Management
2.	Perform quantitative analysis of health records to evaluate compliance with regulations and standards.	Health Records Quality Assessment
3.	Perform qualitative analysis of health records to evaluate compliance.	Health Records Quality Assessment Management
4.	Assist in preparing the facility of an accreditation, licensing and/or certification survey.	All
5.	Ensure facility-wide adherence to health information services' compliance with regulatory requirements (e.g., ICD-9-CM Cooperating parties coding guidelines, CMS Compliance Plan, Correct Coding Initiative).	All

IV. DOMAIN: INFORMATION TECHNOLOGY AND SYSTEMS

A. Subdomain: Information Technology

1.	Use common software packages (e.g., spreadsheets, databases, word processing, graphics, presentation, statistical, e-mail).	Information Systems All
2.	Use electronic/imaging technology to store medical records.	Retention & Retrieval
3.	Query facility-wide databases to retrieve information.	Information Systems Retention & Retrieval Quality Assessment
4.	Generate reports from various databases.	Information Systems Quality Assessment
5.	Protect data integrity and validity of information using software or hardware technology.	Information Systems
6.	Identify common software problems.	Information Systems

B. Subdomain: Health Information Systems		
1.	Collect and report data on incomplete records and timeliness of record completion.	Health Records Management
2.	Maintain filing and retrieval systems for paper-based patient records.	Retention & Retrieval
3.	Maintain integrity of master patient/client index.	Retention & Retrieval
4.	Maintain integrity of patient numbering and filing systems.	Retention & Retrieval
5.	Design forms, computer input screens and other health record documentation tools.	Health Records

V. DOMAIN: ORGANIZATION AND MANAGEMENT

A. Subdomain: Health Information Services Management		
1.	Monitor staffing levels, turnaround time, productivity and workflow.	Financial Management
2.	Determine resources (equipment and supplies) to meet workload needs.	Financial Management
3.	Develop departmental procedures.	Management
4.	Develop strategic plans, goals and objectives for area of responsibility.	Management
5.	Participate in intra-departmental teams/committees.	Management
6.	Participate in facility-wide teams/committees responsible for health information services issues.	Management
7.	Provide consultation, education and training to users of health information services.	Management
8	Use quality improvement tools and techniques to improve departmental processes.	Management Quality Assessment
9.	Plan and conduct meetings.	Management
10.	Resolve customer complaints.	Management
11.	Prioritize department functions and services.	Management
12.	Implement staff orientation and training programs.	Management
13.	Manage special projects	Management

BLUEPRINT OF THE RHIT REGISTRATION EXAM

There are 46 task/competency statements for RHIT. As stated previously in this guide, the certification exam questions are based on these statements. The chart and table below are graphic visualizations of the percentages and number of exam questions that correlate to each of the subdomains. This will give a better understanding of the emphasis placed on a subdomain in relation to an exam question. This way, study endeavors can be planned accordingly.

Percentage of Exam Questions Per Domain

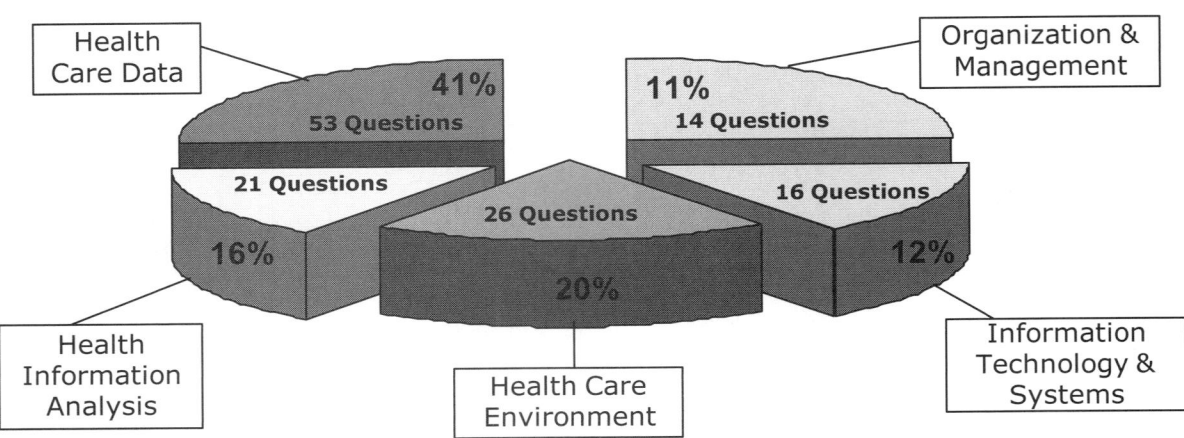

Number of Questions Per Subdomain: RHIA Examination	
Data Structure, Content and Use	27
Clinical Classification Systems ICD-9-CM	13
Clinical Classification Systems CPT/HCPCS	13
Health Care Statistics & Research	21
Health Care Delivery Systems	8
Legal Issues	8
Information Requirements and Standards	10
Information Technology	8
Health Information Systems	8
Organization and Supervision	14

Please note: This breakdown of questions to subdomains does not include the additional 20 questions that are not scored.

RHIT

CROSS INDEX: HEALTH INFORMATION CONTENT AREA TO TASK COMPETENCIES

General Content Areas	Domains, Subdomains, and Task Competencies
Health Records	I.A.1, I.A.2
	II.B.1, II.B.2
	III.A.1, III.A.2, III.C.1, III.C.2, III.C.3, III.C.4, III.C.5
	IV.A.1
Information Retention and Retrieval	III.A.1, III.A.2
	IV.A.1, IV.A.2, IV.A.3, IV.A.4, IV.B.2, IV.B.3, IV.B.4,
Classification and Indexing Systems	I.A.1, I.A.2, I.A.3, I.A.4, I.B.1, I.C.1
	III.A.1, III.A.2, III.C.4, III.C.5
	IV.A.1
Coding	I.B.1, I.C.1
	III.A.1, III.A.2, III.C.4, III.C.5
	IV.A.1
Medical Sciences	I.A.2, I.A.4
	III.A.1, III.A.2, III.C.4, III.C.5
	IV.A.1
Statistics and Research	II.A.4, II.A.5
	III.A.1, III.A.2, III.C.4, III.C.5
	IV.A.1
Quality Assessment and Improvement	I.A.2, I.A.4
	II.A.2, II.A.3, II.A.4, II.A.5
	III.A.1, III.A.2, III.C.2, III.C.3, IIII.C.4, III.C.5
	IV.A.3, IV.A.4
	V.A.8
Health Law	III.A.1, III.A.2, III.B.1, III.B.2, III.B.3, III.B.4, III.C.4, III.C.5
	IV.A.1
Information Systems	I.A.2
	II.B.1
	III.A.1, III.A.2, III.C.4, III.C.5
	IV.A.1, IV.A.3, IV.A.4, IV.A.5, IV.A.6
Management	III.A.1, III.A.2, III.C.1, III.C.3, III.C.4, III.C.5
	IV.A.1, IV.B.
	V.A.1, V.A.3, V.A.4, V.A.5, V.A.6, V.A.7, V.A.8, V.A.9, V.A.10, V.A.11, V.A.12, V.A.13
Human Resources	III.A.1, III.A.2, III.C.4, III.C.5
	IV.A.1
Financial Management	III.A.1, III.A.2, III.C.4, III.C.5
	IV.A.1
	V.A.2

Knowledge and Skill Content Areas

Although AHIMA and the COC no longer identify the knowledge and skill areas that emerge from the Roles and Function Study as they have in the past, they still have an important purpose. For the most part, mastery of these knowledge and skill areas are required to successfully perform the task competencies.

Knowledge Areas

To successfully perform the task competencies, one should be knowledgeable of the following:

K-1	Accreditation standards related to patient-related data (accreditation standards for various types of facilities)
K-2	Federal and state regulations related to patient-related data (regulations for various types of facilities)
K-3	Budgeting (i.e. budget types, procedures, principles)
K-4	Managerial accounting
K-5	Work measurement and analysis
K-6	Professional practice standards (i.e. AHIMA and other related data for regulations for various types of facilities)
K-7	Quality control techniques
K-8	Disease process
K-9	Language of medicine (i.e. medical terminology)
K-10	Office ergonomics
K-11	Safety standards (i.e. OSHA, state, Joint Commission, etc.)
K-12	Legal requirements for confidentiality of patient-related data (federal and sate)
K-13	Medical record content
K-14	Record/information control systems
K-15	Vital statistics (i.e. state federal regulations and procedures for collection and reporting)

K-16	Communication techniques
	    oral: interpersonal, small group, professional speaking
	    written: business and professional writing

K-17	Record filing systems
K-18	Health related facility organizations
K-19	Healthcare facility committees (i.e. medical staff, administrative including Medical Record, Quality Improvement, Risk Management, etc.)
K-20	Business/committee procedures and rules of order
K-21	Case mix systems(i.e. DRGs, APACHE)
K-22	Medical nomenclatures and diagnostic classification systems (i.e. ICD-9-CM, CPT, HCPCS, DSM, etc.)
K-23	Data verification techniques
K-24	PRO standards and procedures
K-25	Statistical techniques
K-26	Data presentation techniques
K-27	Research Design
K-28	Computer statistical packages (i.e. SPSS, SAS. etc.)
K-29	Principles/methods for assigning patient care quality and effectiveness
K-30	Principles/methods for assessing resources for patient care
K-31	Principles/methods of risk management
K-32	Management principles of planning and organizing

K-33	Functions related to Medical Record, Utilization Management, Quality Improvement, Cancer Registry and related departments
K-34	Management principles of controlling
K-35	Business and professional writing techniques
K-36	Principles of job analysis
K-37	General system principles
K-38	Work simplification techniques
K-39	Forms design and management
K-40	Information technologies
K-41	Systems analysis design, development and implementation principles
K-42	Project planning
K-43	Data security techniques (manual and computer)
K-44	Space management
K-45	Methods/procedures for procurement, maintenance and selection of equipment and supplies
K-46	Principles of Human Resources Management
K-47	Principles of organizational behavior
K-48	Cancer staging systems
K-49	Principles of in-service education

Skill Areas

To successfully perform the task competencies, one should be skilled in the following:

S-1   Survey instrument design (i.e. written and interview)
S-2   Interviewing
S-3   Budget development and implementation
S-4   Application of managerial accounting techniques
S-5   Work measurement techniques
S-6   Quality control methods
S-7   Data presentation
S-8   Data collection techniques
S-9   Data analysis
S-10   Interpretation of medical record content
S-11   Implementation of new/revised systems
S-12   Collection & compilation of vital statistics
S-13   Interpersonal and small group communication
S-14   Filing procedures
S-15   Professional speaking and presentation
S-16   Conducting committee business meetings
S-17   Applying principles of diagnostic classification systems
S-18   Applying case-mix algorithms
S-19   Critical thinking
S-20   Applying procedures for assessing patient care quality/effectiveness
S-21   Interpretation of statistical data
S-22   Professional and business writing
S-23   Applying work simplification techniques
S-24   System analysis
S-25   Applying project planning techniques
S-26   Developing presentations for inservice education
S-27   Applying principles of Human Resources Management
        (i.e. selecting, training, motivating, promoting personnel, etc.)
S-28   Cancer staging Systems

Adopted by the
Council on Certification
January 1992

THE GROUNDWORK

I think I can

Many students do not fare well on exams because of stress and test anxiety. The absolute best way to reduce test anxiety and minimize your stress level is to be prepared. Granted, even the most prepared individual can still have episodes of apprehension. Yet, there is no question that stress has a negative consequence on test performance.

OK, so you feel you are prepared, but the anxiety is still interfering with your ability to think. What can you do? There is a direct correlation between the level of test performance and the level of test anxiety. On the up side, a certain amount of anxiety can be positive and necessary. The student that approaches a test without anxiety tends to perform poorly. The trick is to have just enough anxiety to avoid the "cockiness" that can lead to answering questions carelessly, but not too much, so that you don't freeze on questions that appear to be "out of nowhere". As stated earlier, knowledge of the material, or rather over-preparedness, is ultimately the best way to decrease stress levels and test anxiety, but more about that later. There are many other "tricks of the stress" that one can do.

One of the first things you will want to do is develop a positive attitude. Remember the children's story *The Little Engine That Could?* Follow the engine's advice and start repeating to yourself: I think I can, I think I can, I think I can, I know I can, I know I can, I **know I can!**

I DID IT. Positive thinking brings you closer to your goals. If you think you can pass the test, you will pass the test. Do not allow those wicked negative thoughts to sway your convictions.

Remove them immediately every time they try to encroach on your common sense. Have a list of platitudes ready when a negative thought attempts an invasion, pull out your *"If I can't do it no one can."* or *"I can see the light at the end of the tunnel."* or *"Take one step at a time.".* Ask yourself *"Why can't I pass this exam?"* The answer invariably will be, and should be: *"There is no reason I can't pass this exam; all I have to do is stay positive and be prepared."*

Stress reducers

Exercise is an excellent stress reducer. There has been much said about the benefits of exercise. It can greatly assist the "Nervous Nellys". Exercising regularly can eliminate a great amount of the "nervous energy" you may be feeling as you push forward with your study plans. Moreover, exercise can help build a positive attitude. It assists in clearing your mind, making you more mentally alert and in readiness for the stresses of studying. Walking, swimming, or bike riding several times a week can be very effective. Or, maybe this is just the right time to try one of those more exotic exercises like in-line skating, water aerobics or Pilates. The important thing is to begin some type of exercise program now! You will feel the benefits immediately.

Controlled breathing and muscle relaxation are two other stress reduction techniques that are in the same family as exercise. Anxiety tends to bring on shortness of breath which sometimes can further increase your anxiety levels. Your goal is to keep your mind as well as your body in a relaxed state. This can be accomplished by controlling your breathing. To induce a relaxation response by using controlled breathing, start by taking a long deep breath. Slowly release this deep breath, and as you do your other body muscles will relax. Do this repeatedly until you feel you have attained a serene state of mind. This exercise should be practiced regularly, and not just when you feel the momentarily lapses of stress or anxiety. The second technique, muscle relaxation, is really a form of Yoga. Your goal is to relax all muscle groups of the body. To accomplish this, you will need to set aside at least ten minutes of uninterrupted time. Start by lying on the floor in the supine position. (You do know what the supine position is?) Turn the lights down low and begin by contracting and then relaxing each muscle group beginning with your toes. Continue to proceed up the body ending with the head. As each muscle group is contracted and then released, the muscle smoothes out and relaxes. Be careful, you might become so restful you'll fall asleep.

These stress reducing strategies do work. But, in order for the techniques to be effective, you must do them. These techniques and exercises can not only help reduce anxiety for the exam but can also be life long strategies for achieving an over all feeling of self-worth and self-esteem.

An outline for understanding and overcoming test anxiety

I. Problems created by test anxiety
  A. Physical and mental effects
    1. headaches
    2. tense muscles
    3. nausea
    4. crying
    5. feeling angry
    6. feelings of helplessness
  B. Test performance effects
    1. difficulty reading and understanding the exam questions
    2. difficulty organizing your thoughts
    3. difficulty applying higher-level thinking
    4. mental blocking (i.e. going blank on questions)

II. Determine the cause of your anxiety
  A. Lack of preparation is a fundamental cause of test anxiety
    1. Complete a self assessment of your preparation process by answering questions:
      a. Am I managing my time appropriately and efficiently?
      b.   Am I organizing my study materials for easy use?
      c. Am I utilizing appropriate study habits?
      d. Have I created a study schedule?
  B. Worrying about issues that are not relevant
    1. past performance on prior exams
    2. what and how other students are doing
    3. comparing yourself to other students' performances

III. Reduce your level of test anxiety
  A. Be prepared by
    1. studying and knowing material to the point that stress won't interfere with answering questions correctly
    2. applying time management skills (see this section and also the tools in the Appendix for specific skill building activities)
      a. create a study schedule
      b. don't cram
      c. create techniques to avoid procrastination
      d. exercise when feeling lazy
    3. practice test taking techniques when studying with simulated test questions (see following pages)
    4. use study tools (see Appendix)
  B. Avoid cramming
  C. Think positive
    1. build confidence by studying properly
  D. Follow a healthy lifestyle
    1. practice relaxation techniques
    2. exercise regularly
  E. Reward yourself after an effective study session

Playing the test game

As stated earlier, doing well on the exam requires a positive attitude, a suitable level of test anxiety, an extensive review of study material and an ability to strategically think and plan. In addition, there are other preparation activities that must be considered in order to achieve a successful outcome on the exam. First, an understanding of the cognitive levels and their relationship to the test questions is essential. Second, an appreciation of test taking strategies and techniques as well as an ability to apply the techniques when appropriate is useful.

Section 1 discussed the relationship between test questions and the three cognitive levels: recall (or knowledge), application and analysis. This section (Section 2) has a more extensive discussion of the cognitive levels with numerous examples of questions at each of these levels. This section also gives a detailed explanation of test strategies and techniques. Examples of test questions and approaches to responding to unfamiliar questions are also provided. Additionally, you will find an outline that reviews a variety of hints and tips that can be used prior to, as well as, on the test day. A total program, in three phases, is described for initiating, organizing, and sustaining your study preparation. Finally, you will find a summary of test taking strategies, methods of study, and other tips that can make your total study program a success.

What do those cognitive levels mean again?

Previously it was noted that the registration exam questions are constructed utilizing three cognitive thinking levels: recall (or knowledge), application and analysis. An individual uses numerous thinking processes and the registration exam questions must reflect these. These processes are ordered, based on levels of complexity. That is to say, to answer a recall question requires the lowest level of the thinking process, simply recalling the information. On the other hand, to answer an analysis question requires that you revert to the highest level of thinking: comparing and contrasting information, forming judgments and making decisions.

In this section, a more detailed explanation and sample questions of each of the cognitive levels are given. By reviewing these examples you will become more adept with the thinking processes that are involved with answering the registration exam questions. It should be noted that the questions that are used as examples were actual questions that the AHIMA used in prior years' certification guides to illustrate typical test questions. The cognitive level of each sample question was determined by the author.

Let's begin.

Recall or Knowledge Questions

Recall or knowledge questions involve the process of memorization. Memorization is committing information to memory through repetition for recollection at a later time. These types of questions are frequently referred to as recall questions. Knowledge/recall questions simply require you to remember information (example: definitions of health care terms). There are strategies that you can utilize to facilitate the process of memorization. For example, when trying to commit to memory specific content, try to draw on strategies that require the use of your senses rather than simply reading the information. Reciting the information out loud or reviewing it in your mind as you write it down requires the use of your senses. Using various mnemonics is also a helpful method for memorizing content. These strategies will be discussed in more detail later in this section. To do well on these types of questions you must be able to recall facts, definitions, descriptions, formulae, sequences, categories, classifications, theories etc. The following are examples of recall or knowledge questions.

1. The condition established after study to be chiefly responsible for occasioning the admission of the patient to the hospital for care is called the:
   a. Primary diagnosis
   b. Principal diagnosis
   c. Admitting diagnosis
   d. Final diagnosis
   The answer is "b".
   To answer this question correctly, you must be able to recall the definition of principle diagnosis.

2. Which of the following is an ICD-9-CM principal diagnosis code?
   a. V27.0 outcome delivery, single liveborn
   b. V30.0 single liveborn in hospital
   c. E966 assault by cutting and piercing instrument
   d. M9010/0 fibroadenoma, NOS
   The answer is "b".
   To answer this question correctly, you must be able to recall what V, E or M codes are acceptable for a principal diagnosis.

3. The medical record department is moving into a new area. It is estimated that the maximum of records that will be housed is 80,000. Each record is one-half inch thick. Occupancy in the new area costs $7.00 per square foot per year. The department expects to stay in the new space at least ten years. New filing equipment will be purchased. Which of the following would save the most amount of space for filing the records in the new area?
   a. five drawer vertical file cabinets
   b. fixed open shelving
   c. four-drawer lateral file cabinets
   d. movable open shelving
   The answer is "d".
   To answer this question correctly, you must be able to recall the description of the different types of cabinets and match the description to the appropriate cabinet. Also, note that the question provides a lot of unnecessary information that need not be considered to answer the question correctly.

4. In training a new employee, which of the following strategies is most likely to provide an environment for success?
   a. job enlargement
   b. job enrichment
   c. participation on a quality improvement team
   d. positive feedback during learning
   The answer is "d".
   To answer this question correctly, you must be able to recall the facts relating to job-training.

5. The component of the learning theory that states "awards appear to be more effective in producing learning than punishment" is:
   a. active practice
   b. motivation
   c. positive re-enforcement
   d. transfer of learning
   The answer is "c".
   To answer this question correctly, you must be able to match the appropriate term to its definition, which is simply a matter of recall.

6. The contract between the Centers for Medicare and Medicaid Services (CMS) and the Quality Improvement Organization (QIO) specifies the activities the QIO must assess at Medicare participating hospitals is called:
   a. Federal Register
   b. Medicare Conditions of Participation
   c. PRO Letter
   d. Scope of Work (SOW)
   The answer is "d".
   To answer this question, correctly you must be able to recall the definitions for each term in order to match the correct term to its meaning.

7. Validation of billing forms in preparation for a Medicare audit reveals errors in discharge disposition. This element refers to the patient's:
   a. destination at discharge
   b. discharge order
   c. final diagnoses
   d. health status on discharge
   The answer is "a".
   To answer this question correctly, you must be able to recall the different types of discharges.

8. A patient of Dr. Adams, who has not been seen in two years, sees Dr. Adams' partner, Dr. Brown. Dr. Adams and Dr. Brown are two members of a single specialty practice. The patient visit should be coded as a (an):
   a. consultation
   b. established patient
   c. new patient
   d. referred patient
   The answer is "b".
   To answer this question correctly, you must be able to recall the different types of outpatient encounters.

9. A tool used to collect feedback from users of a system process or activity is a:
   a. control chart
   b. customer satisfaction survey
   c. run chart
   d. standards flow chart
   The answer is "b".
   To answer this question correctly, you must be able to identify the different types of charts and forms.

10. To monitor increasing or decreasing staffing needs, a supervisor may utilize a:
    a. task analysis diagram
    b. work distribution chart
    c. work sampling technique
    d. work simplification technique
    The answer is "b".
    To answer this question correctly, you must be able to identify the different types of management tools.

11. Physician suspension data are routinely presented at which committee?
    a. Credentials
    b. Executive
    c. Joint Conference
    d. Quality Assurance
    The answer is "a".
    To answer this question correctly, you must be able to identify the different types of hospital committees.

Application Questions

Before you can start the thinking process that is required to respond to application questions, you must thoroughly understand the information. To begin, you must recall the memorized facts. These facts must then be translated and clarified. If you can accomplish this, you have comprehended the information but not yet applied it. This thinking process must be taken one step further in order to respond correctly to an application question. The process of applying information requires that you remember and comprehend concepts and apply them to specific situations. These concepts can be anything from theories of management to generalizations. It requires that you know, solve, modify, change, use or manipulate the information as it is applied to a "real" circumstance. Application questions challenge your ability to use information under new conditions. The following are examples of application questions.

HOSPITAL INPATIENT CENSUS-SEPTEMBER 9

UNIT	Beds on Unit	Pts MN/9/8	PLUS Adm.	Transfer In	Discharge	MINUS Died	Transfer Out	Pts MN 9/9	PLUS A&D's	InPt Service Days 9/9
S1	25	23	4	1	3	1		24		24
S2	30	29	3		4		1	27	1	28
M1	28	25	5		4		2	24		24
M2	32	26	4	1	3			28		28
PMS	22	20	4	1	3			22		22
ICU	8	5	1	2		1	2	5		5
OB	25	20	2	1	4			19	2	21
P	25	20	2	1	4			19	2	21
PIC	20	16	4		1	1	1	17		17
ECU	30	29	1	1	3			28		28
NN	25	18	3	1	3		1	18		18
TOTAL	270	231	33	9	32	3	7	231	5	236

1. The health information department is responsible for checking the accuracy of statistics calculated from the computer-generated data. What should the inpatient bed occupancy ratio for all inpatients beds and bassinets be on September 9?
   a. 84.4%
   b. 85.5%
   c. 87.4%
   d. 88.3%
   The answer is "c".
   To answer this question correctly, you must be able to recall the formula and definition for inpatient bed occupancy rate and apply it to this situation.

2. Where is the most likely place in an inpatient record to find documentation regarding an unscheduled return to surgery within the same admission for the same condition?
   a. emergency record
   b. physician's orders
   c. post-anesthesia recovery record
   d. progress notes
   The answer is "d".
   To answer this question correctly, you must recall the different types of medical record formats and understand what is used when and apply it to this situation.

Application Questions

3. In conducting a review of laboratory utilization, which one of the following laboratory tests should be ordered with a diagnosis of gout?
    a. Serum Uric Acid Level
    b. Rheumatoid factor (RF)
    c. Blood Calcium Level
    d. Carcinoembryonic Antigen (CEA)
   The answer is "a".
   To answer this question correctly, you must recall the definitions for each lab test and apply the correct one to this situation.

Analysis of Question 3
The clinical features of gout are very distinctive. An elevated serum urate content supports the diagnosis and differentiates gout from septic joint and rheumatoid arthritis.

4. The following are objectives of space management, EXCEPT:
    a. to develop workflow effectively
    b. to locate all management personnel together
    c. to permit flexibility to rearrange area
    d. to use space most efficiently
   The answer is "b".
   To answer this question correctly, you must to understand the basics of space management and apply them to this situation.

5. A key to continuous quality improvement is:
    a. do it right the first time
    b. find the poor performers and take action
    c. inspect, find problem and take action
    d. solve each problem as it is encountered
   The answer is "a".
   To answer this question correctly, you must recall knowledgeable of the CQI process and apply it to this situation.

*Application
Questions*

6. A patient is a known non-insulin dependent diabetic admitted for pneumonia. A sputum culture revealed Group A streptococcus pneumonia. Admission glucose was 180. The patient was treated with Diabinese and antibiotics. On discharge, the physician documents the diagnoses as "Streptococcus pneumonia; Diabetes mellitus." The correct coding and sequencing is:
   a. 482.31   Pneumonia, due to streptococcus, Group A
      250.00   Diabetic without mention of complication, Type II
   b. 486   Pneumonia, Organism, unspecified
      041.01   Streptococcus, Group A
      250.00   Diabetic without mention of complication, Type II
   c. 482.31   Pneumonia, due to streptococcus, Group A
      250.90   Diabetes, uncontrolled, Type II
   d. 486   Pneumonia, Organism unspecified
      041.01   Streptococcus, Group A
      250.90   Diabetes, uncontrolled, Type II
   The answer is: "a".
   To answer this question correctly, you must recall the disease processes, the coding conventions and together apply them to this situation.

7. Which of the following terms describes the calculation that shows how much variation there is in a set of data?
   a. mean
   b. percentage
   c. ratio
   d. standard deviation
   The answer is "d".
   To answer this question correctly, you must recall the definitions of the terms and apply them to this situation.

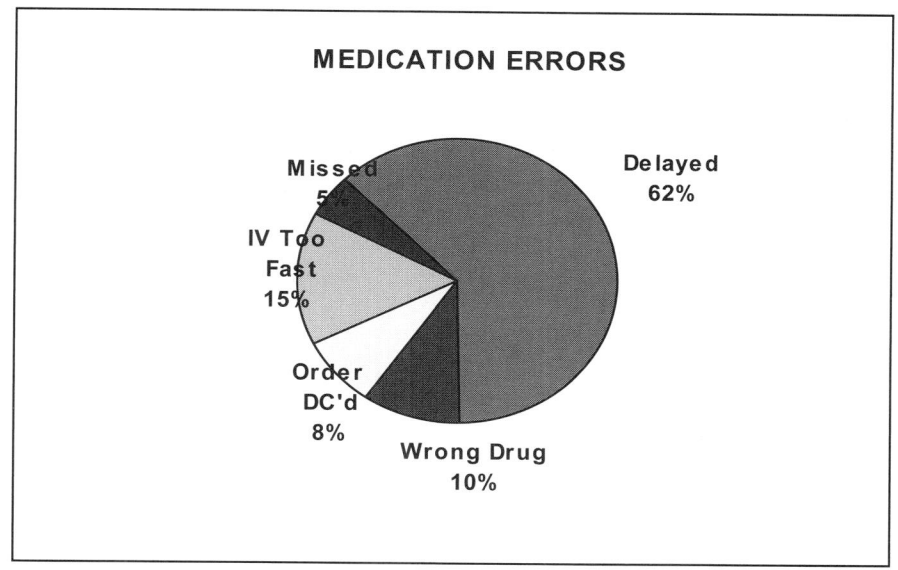

8. The graph shown above is a useful way of presenting information for what quality management purpose?
   a. Explaining proportions of each element relative to the total study population
   b. Showing all steps in a process in order to identify areas for potential improvement
   c. Tracking results of a procedure over a period of time to look for trends
   d. Understanding how a process functions and for monitoring variations in that process.
   The answer is "a".
   To answer this question correctly, you must recall the generalizations regarding graphs and determine what would apply in this situation.

9. In reference to work station ergonomics, the most frequent occurring job-related disorder is:
   a. carpal tunnel syndrome
   b. dysarthria
   c. hyperhidrosis
   d. Raynaud syndrome
   The answer is "a".
   To answer this question correctly, you must recall and understand the disease processes and apply them to this situation.

10. The best approach in developing a request for proposal (RFP) for a new chart tracking system is to:
    a. be very general about the needs of the new system
    b. delay distribution until a vendor is selected
    c. include as great a degree of specification as possible
    d. provide only information on functional capabilities desired

    The answer is "c".

    To answer this question correctly, you must recall the definition and understand the components of an RFP and then apply that information to this situation.

11. Discharge as a form of discipline is justified if an employee
    a. is tardy by more than 15 minutes on a regular basis
    b. knowingly falsified information on the employment application
    c. occasionally drops below established performance
    d. shows discourtesy towards fellow employees

    The answer is "b".

    To answer this question correctly, you must recall the principles of discipline progression and apply them to this situation.

12. Within the life cycle of a computer system, the development and implementation process is often staged:
    a. after analysis of the current environment
    b. between alpha and beta testing
    c. in a meeting with key staff members
    d. over a number of months or years

    The answer is "d".

    To answer this question correctly, you must recall the information relating to system life cycle and apply them to this situation.

Analysis Questions

Analysis questions require your highest level of thinking. They are based on your ability to interpret the information, understand the likes and differences of the information and understand how all the information relates to the presented situation. Your ability to respond correctly to an analysis question is directly related to your ability to respond to recall and application questions. If you do not recall the information or you are unable to apply the information, you will have a very difficult time evaluating and interpreting the information and then making a judgment or decision based on that evaluation. Analysis questions test your analytical abilities. These abilities are needed when making decisions, judgments or solving problems.

Analysis
Questions

Based on the scenario below, answer question 1
The medical record department is moving into a new area. It is estimated that a maximum of 80,000 records will be housed. Each record is one-half inch thick. Occupancy in the new area costs $7.00 per square foot per year. The department expects to stay in the new space at least ten years. New filing equipment will be purchased.

1. If fixed open-shelf files require aisle space of 882 square feet for the entire file area, how many total feet of floor space will be required for the projected number of records housed in units that are 3 feet wide, 1 foot deep and 6 shelves high?
   a. 558
   b. 1,440
   c. 1,993
   d. 2,976

The answer is "b".
To answer this question correctly, you must recall the mathematical equation that is required, break down the elements and perform the calculations to solve the problem. Note: The question contains information that is not relevant to solving the problem.

Analysis of Question 1
Several steps are required in order to solve this problem.
1. Determine the square feet of the shelves:
   3 ft. wide x 1 ft. long = 3 sq. ft. (W x L = SQ FT)
2. Determine how many files per sq. in. there are:
   80,000 records x .5 (thickness of records) = 40,000 files
3. Determine how many shelving units are needed:
   a. 36 inch (3 ft wide) x 6 shelves high = 216 inches per unit
   b. 40,000 records (answer from step 2) ÷ 216 inches = 185.1 units = 186 units needed. Remember units must always be rounded up.
4. Determine how many SQF each unit requires.
   Calculation: 3 SQF (answer from step 1) x 186 units = 558 SQF
5. Add units SQF to SQF required for aisles.
   Calculation: 882+558 = 1,440 SQF needed

**Analysis
Questions**

2. The cardiac care unit has 12 patient beds. There were 3,167 patient days of care provided in the year. What is the cardiac unit's percentage of occupancy?
   a. 8.7%
   b. 72.3%
   c. 11.5%
   d. 26.3%

   The answer is "b".
   To answer this question correctly, you must recall the definition of patient days, the bed count and the formula for occupancy rates. Then you must break down the elements and perform the calculations to solve the problem.

   Analysis of Question 2
   The formula for occupancy rate is: number of patient days divided by number of bed count times days in period.
   The equation is: 3,167 ÷ 12 x 365 = 72.3%

3. A coding backlog of 1,350 charts exists. Department productivity standards call for coding an average of four charts per hour. How many temporary FTEs will need to be employed to eliminate the backlog in two weeks? To be considered a full time employee, the employee must work 8 hours a day, 5 days a week.
   a. 4.2 FTEs
   b. 8.4 FTEs
   c. 9.6 FTEs
   d. 16.9 FTEs

   The answer is "a".
   To answer this question correctly, you must recall and understand issues related to productivity standards, break down the elements and calculate the formula required to solve the problem.

   Analysis of Question 3
   If the productivity standard is four charts an hour, then you must be determine how many charts can be done in an 8-hour day.
   Calculation: 4 charts x 8 hours = 32
   There are 10 working days.
   Calculation: 32 x 10 = 320
   There are 1,350 charts that are backlogged which will require 320 hours to complete.
   Calculation: 1,350 ÷ 320 = 4.2 FTEs

Analysis
Questions

4. The department's first quarter budget analysis shows that while the expected operations cost $337,195, the actual operations cost was $346,207. The budget variance is:
   a. 1.0%
   b. 2.7%
   c. 3.4%
   d. 5.0%

   The answer is "b".
   To answer this question correctly, you must recall the principles involved with budgets. You must understand what is meant by budget variances and know the formula for budget variance. Then complete the calculations to solve the problem.

   Analysis of Question 4
   The formula for budget variance is the actual budget less the planned budget divided by the planned budget equals the budget variance.
   $346,207 - $337,195 ÷ $337,195 = 2.7%

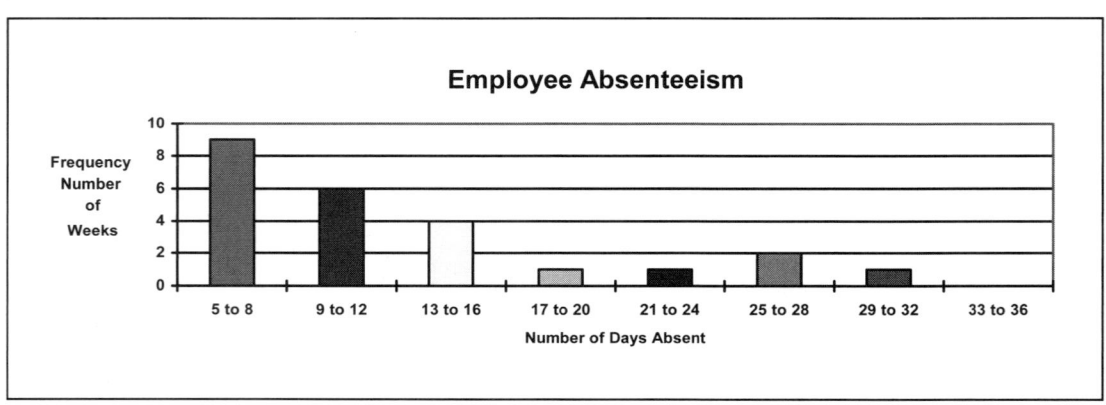

5. From the graph on employee absenteeism, what is the range in number of days absent from work?
   a. 0 to 9
   b. 5 to 8
   c. 5 to 32
   d. 8 to 33

   The answer is "c".
   To answer this question correctly, you are not required to perform any calculations, but you must interpret and differentiate the information in order to make the correct decision.

Analysis
Questions

	RANK	VENDOR A		VENDOR B		VENDOR C		VENDOR D	
		RATING	WEIGHT	RATING	WEIGHT	RATING	WEIGHT	RATING	WEIGHT
QUALITY	5	4		3		3		2	
SPEED	4	3		1		4		2	
MAINTENANCE	2	3		3		5		2	
SERVICE	3	5		2		4		3	
UPGRADE	3	4		3		4		3	
SIZE	2	5		3		3		1	
TOTAL WEIGHT									
PURCHASE PRICE/LIST COST		$18,000		$10,000		$12,000		$2,500 Per year for 5 years	

6. The cost/benefit information on new equipment has been collected. In reviewing the table above, from which vendor should purchase be recommended?
   a. vendor a
   b. vendor b
   c. vendor c
   d. vendor d

The answer is "c" (Vendor C).
To answer this question correctly, you are required to perform specific calculations, after which an analysis and judgment is done to correctly answer the question.

Analysis of Question 6
Completing the benefit analysis reveals that:
   Vendor A is valued at 75 points
   Vendor B at 45 points
   Vendor C at 68 points
   Vendor D at 48 points.
Justification can be made for equipment costing slightly more than the lowest for benefits that are second highest. Vendor C offers the best cost/benefit combination.

DRG xxx-reimbursement amount $3,000

PHYSICIAN	NUMBER OF PATIENTS	AVERAGE COST/CASE	ACTUAL COST
A	33	$2,995	$98,835
B	20	$3,015	$60,300
C	5	$3,075	$15,375
D	40	$3,010	$120,400

7. From the case mix analysis above, which physician is the hospital's biggest overall loser?
   a. Physician A
   b. Physician B
   c. Physician C
   d. Physician D

The answer is "d".
To answer this question correctly, you are required to perform minor calculations, after which an analysis and judgment is done to correctly answer the question.

Analysis of Question 7
Physician A's cost is $5 less than the DRG reimbursement amount so he is a winner.
Physician B's cost is $15 over the reimbursement amount so at 20 patients he has lost a total of $300 for the hospital.
Physician C has lost a total of $375
Physician D has lost a total of $400.

Table 1

Alternatives	Purchase Price	Total Square Feet Required	Life Expectancy in Years
ALTERNATIVE I	$50,220	1,488	10
ALTERNATIVE II	$40,032	1,688	10
ALTERNATIVE III	$26,114	1,784	7
ALTERNATIVE IV	$57,024	924	5

8. A medical record department is moving to a new area. Occupancy in the new area costs $7.00 per square foot per year. The department expects to stay for 10 years. The manger of the department has been given approval to purchase new filing equipment. In order to make an appropriate decision about which filling equipment is the most cost effective, the following information has been collected (see TABLE 1 above). Although there may be other information that would be of value in making a final decision, use the information provided to determine which alternative is most effective.
   a. ALTERNATIVE I
   b. ALTERNATIVE II
   c. ALTERNATIVE III
   d. ALTERNATIVE IV

The answer is "d".
To answer this question, you must complete calculations on each of the alternatives. Also, it must be realized that the "Life Expectancy in Years" column is not relevant to the decision. After the calculations and analysis of the information is completed, a decision can be made.

Analysis of Question 8
The scenario states that the new area will cost the department $7.00 per square foot and the department expects to remain in this space for at least ten years. Therefore, this information must be included in the calculations. The square footage of each alternative is multiplied by the $7.00, and this product is multiplied by 10 years. The purchase price is then added to that product. The answer obtained from the last calculation is the one that is used as a comparison. Thus:
Alternative I:
1,488 x $7.00 = $10,416
$10,416 x 10 years = $104,106
$104,106 + $50,220 (Alternative I purchase price) = $154,380
(This means that over 10 years, it will cost the department $154,380 if this alternative is chosen.)
The above series of calculations is performed for each alternative. Based on each answer, comparisons are made and a decision as to the most cost effective alternative is formulated.

I went the wrong way

This information may seem basic and fundamental, but many times students forget or ignore their importance leading to a negative outcome on exams.

The first test component that offers vital information is the directions. Remember, the questions themselves are a form of directions, so read carefully and critically.

People frequently fail tests **NOT** because they lack the knowledge or the ability but because they did not follow the directions properly.

It is not uncommon to have 2 answers on a multiple choice test in which both appear to be correct. The decision as to which option is correct should be based on the situation given in the question and what would be **best** under those circumstances. In other words, choose the option that **best** answers the question.

Since you are not penalized for an incorrect guess, it is in your best interest to answer all questions. A random guess has a 25% chance of being correct.

Set up a time schedule before you begin the test.
  RHIA: There are a total of 160 questions plus 20 un-scored questions
  RHIT: There are a total of 130 questions plus 20 un-scored questions

Multiple Choice Questions:
  amount of time allotted
  number of test items

$$RHIA = \frac{240 \text{ minutes (4 hours)}}{160 \text{ questions} + 20 \text{ un-scored}} = 1.33 \text{ minutes per question}$$

$$RHIT = \frac{210 \text{ minutes}}{130 \text{ questions} + 20 \text{ un-scored}} = 1.4 \text{ minutes per question}$$

It is not unusual to see a chart, table, graph, case history or description of a situation used as a question. You must still look for the best response. Sometimes these can be the easiest questions, especially the tables and graphs, but students tend to become unnecessarily intimidated by them.

I have no idea what they are talking about

The following are ELIMINATION techniques that can be applied when the correct answer is unknown. After reading the exam question, the flow of the question may help to point to the correct answer. Note: Only apply these techniques when the answer is unknown.

Elimination Technique #1: The stem clue

With the "stem clue" it is possible to identify the correct answer through its relationship to the exam question itself (stem). This relationship can be in the form of:
- an exact repetition of one or more words
- repetition of part of word
- a word with the same meaning

1. Which of the following tasks would be the most appropriate for the Medical Record/HIM Director to delegate to the Supervisor of Record Processing and Statistics?
   a. formulation of a record retention policy for the entire facility
   ☑ b. review of monthly statistical reports to verify accuracy
   c. interviewing applicants for the position of Tumor Registrar
   d. completion of a performance rating on the Assistant Director of the department

   Answer "b" contains the word "statistical", which is a repetition the word form statistics, which is used in the stem.

2. Hypertrophy of the left ventricle may be due to:
   a. cor pulmonale
   ☑ b. systemic <u>hypertension</u>
   c. constrictive carditis
   d. CHF without cardiomegaly

   Answer "b" contains the word "hypertension", which is a repetition of part of the word form hypertrophy, which is used in the stem.

3. A supervisor would use work simplification to:
    a. set standards of performance
    b. speed up employee motions
    c. measure employee productivity
  ☑ d. devise easier ways of doing things

Answer "d" contains the word "easier", which means the same thing as "simplification" which is used in the stem.

GOALS FOR CITY HOSPITAL	
DEPARTMENT	GOAL
Administrative	Develop a comprehensive QA plan
Medical Record Department	Perform a QI study on coding
Coding Supervisor	Monitor and follow-up coding procedures

4. This hospital is practicing:
    a. span of control
  ☑ b. management by objectives
    c. zero-based budgeting
    d. cash budgeting

Answer "b" contains the word "objectives", which is similar in meaning to the word "goal" which is used in the stem.

5. Adenocarcinoma is a malignant neoplasm arising from:
    a. adipose tissue
    b. cartilage tissue
  ☑ c. glandular tissue
    d. smooth muscle tissue

Answer "c" contains the word "glandular", which means the same as "adeno" in the word adenocarcinoma which is used in the stem.

6. The most common budgetary approach that is utilized and is based on a fixed annual level of volume activity is known as:
    a. zero-based budgeting
    b. a variable budget
    c. a flexible budget
  ☑ d. a fixed or target budget

Answer "d" contains the word "fixed", which is a repetition of the word "fixed" which is used in the stem.

Elimination Technique #2: The related or unrelated clue

With the "related or unrelated clue", it is possible to determine the correct answer by eliminating answers that are alike. If two or more answers are similar, they can be eliminated since they all can't be correct.

1. The hectoquadric logarithm of 580 is equal to:
   a. 2^3
   ☑ b. 7
   c. 8
   d. square root of 64

   Answers "a", "c" and "d" are related since they all mean the same thing, and thus can be eliminated.

2. As director of the health information department, you are planning some changes in the workflow to increase efficiency. Your first step should be to:
   a. make a PERT network of the new workflow
   ☑ b. make a movement diagram of the current workflow
   c. draw a Pareto chart depicting reasons the current system is inefficient
   d. complete a decision matrix to determine which type of new equipment to purchase.

   Answers "a" and "b" both contain the word, "work flow", which is a repetition of the word "work flow" that is used in the stem, and thus "c" and "d" can be eliminated which will increase your chances of guessing the correct response by 50%.

3. The development of the fetus continues in the:
   ☑ a. uterus
   b. salpinx
   c. fallopian tubes
   d. cervix

   Answers "b" & "c" are related since they mean the same thing, and thus can be eliminated.

4. An evaluation of the number of WBC is called a (an):
   a. erythrocyte count
   ☑ b. leukocyte count
   c. RBC count
   d. thrombocyte count

   Answers "a" and "c" are related since they mean the same thing, and thus can be eliminated.

Elimination Technique #3: The absurd clue

With the "absurd clue" it is possible to determine the correct answer by eliminating answers that are logically inconsistent with the question. The answer that is eliminated is not necessarily absurd, but in context of the question, appears illogical.

1. What body system contains the colon?
☑ a. digestive
   b. respiratory
   c. chest x-ray
   d. CAT scan

   Answers "c" and "d" are absurd since they are obviously not body systems, and thus can be eliminated.

Elimination Technique #4: The absolute cue

With the "absolute clue" it is possible to determine the correct answer by eliminating answers that contain specific determiners, words that imply always, never etc..

1. Osteoarthritis:
   a. can only be confirmed with a positive RA test
☑ b. is considered to be a degenerative disease
   c. means the same thing as Ricketts
   d. is curable most of the time

   Answers "a" and "d" contain words that are absolute determiners, and thus can probably be eliminated.

2. With regards to treatment and consent for treatment, patients:
☑ a. can refuse treatment, even when their life is endanger
   b. are never given a copy of the signed consent form
   c. who have children, but are underage cannot give consent for themselves
   d. must be able to sign the consent form with a proper signature

   Answer "b" contains the word, "never", which is an absolute determiner, and thus can probably be eliminated.

Elimination technique #5: The rational clue

With the "rational clue" it is possible to determine the correct answer by thinking it through in a basic logical fashion. Try and determine what you do know about the question, break it down into parts and then eliminate.

1. You have been requested to assist in the planning and organizing of a data security program at your hospital for computerized information. Evaluate the following data security measures and determine which would be considered the most appropriate.
   a. user codes, locks on the terminals and *flow charts*
   b. passwords, identification cards and *data banks*
   ☑ c. passwords, user codes and close monitoring of all inquiries
   d. *flow charts, data banks* and close monitoring of all inquiries

   In answer "c", all of the items relate to security, where the others do not, i.e. the italicized words do not relate to security measures.

2. Most POMR records file operative data chronologically. Which is the preferred sequence in this method?
   ☑ a. consent, anesthesia, operative report, path report
   b. operative report, anesthesia, consent, path report
   c. anesthesia, operative report, path report, consent
   d. operative report, consent, anesthesia, path report

   Answer "a" list the forms according to the chronology in which each event took place;
   • first the consent was obtained
   • then the anesthesia was given for the operation
   • the operation was followed by the dictated report
   • and finally the path report is sent to the floor

   This decision is best made on sound logical and rational thought.

3. In order to graphically portray the functions performed in a cancer registry system, one would need to do a:
   a. systems analysis
   b. job description
   c. process flowchart
   ☑ d. systems flowchart

   Even though response "a" has the word "system", the word "analysis" certainly is not related to a graphic representation, where as response "d" has the word" system" and "flowchart" which is a graphic representation.

4. Five major components of forms design are:
☑ a. heading, introduction, instructions, body and closing
   b. paper cost, instructions, heading, page and identification
   c. edition date, heading, instructions
   d. paper cost, heading, instructions

Some of the responses in answers "b", "c" and "d" have nothing to do with the design of forms such as paper cost and edition date. Note: When attempting to answer a question that has a listing of answers per response, if one answer in the response is wrong, the whole answer is wrong.

Elimination Technique #6: The true-false clue

With the "true-false clue", it is possible to determine the correct answer by thinking of the question as a series of true or false statements. This approach is particularly helpful when you experience a mental block about the format of the multiple choice question.

1. The inpatient's record begins in the:
☑ a. admitting department
   b. patient's room
   c. nursing station
   d. physician's office

Answer C is the only true statement
   T or F   The inpatient's record begins in the admitting department.
   T or F   The inpatient's record begins in the patient's room.
   T or F   The inpatient's record begins in the nursing station.
   T or F   The inpatient's record begins in the physician's office.

Looking For Clues

An outline of test taking tactics

I. **Timing**
   A. Pace yourself.
      1. There is a time button on the computer monitor which will indicate remaining time.
   B. Recognize time consuming questions.
   C. RHIA EXAM:
      1. You will have 4 hours to complete the exam.
      2. There are a total of 160 questions that will comprise your score plus an additional 20 questions that are not scored. (Please check your certification guide or AHIMA's web page for the most current information.)
   D. RHIT EXAM:
      1. You will have 3½ hours to complete the exam.
      2. There will be a total of 130 questions that will comprise your score plus an additional 20 questions that are not scored. (Please check your certification guide or AHIMA's web page for the most current information.)

II. **Practice Exams**
   A. Simulate the exam using any practice tests you may have. Your exam practice will be more effective if you have access to computer-simulated exams.
      1. Time yourself.
      2. Avoid interruptions (e.g. phone, TV, etc.).

III. **Organize your studying**
   A. Study in groups
      1. Group study is especially helpful when tackling your weak areas.
      2. Assign each other specific topics to present and then instruct one another.
      3. Each member of the study team brings his/her individual strengths to share so all can benefit from the alliance.
   B. Use a study journal (see Appendix I).
      1. Note important points in your journal, reference them to the text and write down the pages where the information can be found.
      2. Keep short notes.
   C. As you review each content area, make up fact sheets of information. Include your areas of strengths and weaknesses (see Appendix VII).
      1. Review the fact sheet regularly.

An outline of test taking tactics

IV. How to Approach Exam Questions

A. Answer the easier questions first. The testing software will allow you to go back and make changes as long as you have available time and/or have not exited the exam.
   1. Do not waste time on unfamiliar or difficult questions. Skip them and return to them when you have completed the exam.

B. When reading the questions:
   1. Answer the easier questions first.
      a. It helps build confidence.
      b. It gains time for harder questions.
   2. Look for the central idea of each question. What is the main point?
   3. Anticipate the answer and then look for it.
   4. Read all of the choices since they can provide clues for the correct answer.
   5. Be aware that the first choice that seems correct may be incorrect. A latter choice may be MORE correct.
   6. Read the question as is.
      a. Don't look for tricky interpretations and miss the obvious.
      b. Avoid over-analyzing or over-simplifying.
   7. Re-read all questions containing negative words. They can be confusing and easily misinterpreted.
   8. Using your own words, rephrase difficult questions.
   9. Stick to the topic of the question. If you don't recognize the other options, they could be decoys.
   10. Be mindful of long answers. For example, if one choice is longer than the others, don't ignore it. It could be right or very wrong.
      a. The longer more inclusive answer tends to be the correct one.
   11. Be alert to absolute, categorical or qualified statements.
      a. Absolutes (all, none, never, etc.) are typically untrue.
      b. Generalizations are generally only partially true.
      c. Qualifiers (more, some, usually, sometimes, etc.) are more likely to be true.
      d. The broader the statement, the more likely it is untrue.
   12. Be aware of answers that may be distracters (answers that take one's attention away from the obvious answer).
      a. unfamiliar terms or phrases
      b. jokes or insults
      c. very high or very low numbers
   13. If two options are alike except for one word, it is likely that the answer is one of those two options.
   14. If the question is long and complex, underline the subject and verb to help you.

An outline of test taking tactics

C. Question Elimination is the art of ruling out wrong answers.
  1. Recognizing wrong answers is a skill and it takes practice.
  2. To recognize wrong answers:
     a. Always read all responses first before making your choice.
     b. Eliminate worst responses narrowing the choices available.
     c. Answer by picking the best response.
  3. As the elimination of wrong answers increases, the odds of choosing the correct answer increases.
  4. A positive choice is more likely to be correct than a negative one.
D. Answer every question.
  1. You are not penalized for answering a question incorrectly.
  2. There is a minimum chance of 25% that you will get it right by guessing.
  3. Use elimination techniques to increase your odds (see Elimination Techniques earlier in this section).
  4. Don't look for a pattern in the answers.
     a. Correct answers are generally in randomized order, not a pattern.
     b. Don't be diverted from your best judgment because you entered three "B" answers in a row.
     c. Stick with your first chosen response unless you are positive it is the wrong choice.
     d. If you have a memory lapse or "block" on a question, go to the next question and return to it later. A later question may trigger your memory.
  5. Resist the temptation to change an answer unless you are certain it is incorrect.
E. You will receive a scratch paper to use.
  1. You are allowed to write on notepaper that is given to you but it must be returned upon completion of exam.
  2. Use the paper to:
     a. Keep track of your thoughts when answering difficult questions.
     b. Write down options you have eliminated.
     c. Track questions you want to return to upon completion of test.

**An outline of
test taking
tactics**

V. Test day

A. Get a good night's sleep - not too much or too little.
B. Eat light before the test. Don't compete with your digestive tract for energy.
C. Be careful of fluid intake prior to test.
   1. If you need to leave the room (i.e. to visit the bathroom), you lose the time it takes.
D. Wear loose and comfortable clothes and bring a sweater to put on or take off in case the room is too cold or too hot.
E. Make a trial run to the test center to determine the best route.
   1. Rushing because you did not allow enough time for transportation can bring on anxiety.
F. Be too early and bring:
   1. enough pencils or pens (you will be given paper there that you can use and then the paper must be returned at end of exam)
   2. a calculator
   3. a picture ID
   4. your test entry card

Follow the yellow brick road

Chronological Approach

It has been said that you can't cram for a standardized test. That is, you can't condense several years of study into a few weeks or months. What you can do is organize a study program that is structured in a way that will allow for an efficient and effective review of content. A structural approach will aid you in learning and retaining the information that is necessary for successful passage of the registration exam. The following is a three phase chronological approach for a successful study program.

Phase 1: Three months before the exam – organize the content

Review all of your study materials: course syllabi, outlines, notes, tests and textbooks. Identify the material that you think will be the most beneficial for your studying purposes. After you have made your choices, start a reading/study journal (see Appendix I) for each health information content area, topic or domain/subdomain/task competency statement. In the journal, note important points or concepts from the material and note where the information can be found. These notes should be as short as possible, sometimes as little as a single word, just enough to clearly indicate the area you will need to review. Your journal should be kept near you whenever you are studying. Every week allow time to examine your journal and review the content you have referenced. When you come across content that you don't remember or understand, read it a second time. At the end of the three months, you will have mastered all areas of weakness. Appendix II is also a helpful tool for this process. Other activities you may want to do to further improve your study outcome are to:

1. Organize all the work that needs to be done and create a schedule for yourself. This will help you to stay on track. A sample schedule is provided. See Appendix III.

2. Make a list of all the tasks that need to be completed. Assign priorities based on the tasks and do the most important ones first. Construct a chart to organize a time frame for your studying (i.e. a Gantt chart or a "To Do List"). See Appendix IV, V and VI.

3. Organize a study group. Assign each other topics and then instruct one another on that topic. Write potential test questions related to your assigned topic. Although there are many different approaches to studying, group study can be very effective. Each individual of the group will bring their area of expertise and all can gain from the collective collaboration. Even if you have never studied in groups before, or prefer not to study with others, it is advisable to spend at least some of your study efforts with a group. See appendices for study group guidance and tools.

Phase 2: One month before the exam – review the content

It is time to review the material that has been identified from Phase 1 as important and necessary for your exam preparation. Using all the information from your study journal, revise the study journal based on the identification of content areas that you feel need to be emphasized. Divide these into segments or categories that are short enough to review in a night's reading. While you are reading, highlight the information that still is a concern. Use that information to begin a more intensive study. Construct a new time chart with the revised information.

Phase 3: Two weeks before the exam – cram

Make a fact sheet from your revised study journal of the 25 most important points that you need to emphasize. See Appendix VII. Read this list whenever possible, at least three to four times a day. Two days before the exam, revise the fact sheet to the 10 most important points. Although reviewing these 10 points may not make a fundamental difference, it can help to prevent the "I just went blank" syndrome that frequently occurs when taking tests.

Any more clues?

Additional considerations

The key to a successful passage of the certification exam is to be aware of all your options. Examine the various study methodologies and strategies. Base your approach on your personal schedule, budget, skills, strengths, weaknesses and preferred learning style. On the following pages are guidelines and suggestions that may be helpful in leading you toward your goal. These study techniques will help to strengthen your critical thinking abilities and reinforce learning.

When should I study?

Study according to your body clock. Determine when you study best. Are you a morning person or are you nocturnal in your habits? Our biological clocks are all different, so take advantage and study when your "clock" tells you. Of course, it may not be possible to always study when your "clock" rings in view of other obligations you may have. If you must study at a less desirable time, do the following before you begin:
- Let the blood run to your head by lifting your feet
- Take some slow deep breaths
- Eat a little something sweet
- Do light exercise for ten minutes

How should I study?

When you are studying, take your notes with a purpose. As you write use key words or phrases. Don't just copy down the information. Your goal is to obtain a few key points from your supplementary materials, notes and texts. Remember, a key point can be an answer to an exam question. Once you have your key points, make up your own exam questions based on these items. The test makers of the exam use the task competencies as their key points to create the exam questions, so you should do the same thing. Use your journal notes and your texts to construct exam questions.

How long should each study session be?

Research has shown that we learn more in three 30 minute sessions than one two hour session. To do this you must have the study material organized. It is extremely important to have all content areas that you intend to examine organized in a practical and orderly manner. Use some of the suggested tools in the Appendix section of this manual to arrange the information in a style that will work best for you. Study time does not include preparation time and you need to be "in readiness" to study effectively and efficiently.

How can I kick-start my study session?

Try to get in a high spirited mood before you begin a study session. Read something that makes you laugh and get into a happy frame of mind. A good mood creates a better learning environment. Good feelings stimulate thought processes and cue the release of learned information from your memory. Remember:

- ❏ Find out when you study best
- ❏ Surround yourself with the appropriate environment
- ❏ Keep a positive frame of mind

Is my method of study active or passive?

Passive study is simply reading and re-reading the material that you think is important. Most passive study is a waste of time since you are not checking yourself. You need to do more than just think about what the answer is. You can learn almost twice as fast if you read, write and listen instead of just reading and trying to memorize. For example, an active study session might first begin by integrating your notes, text and supplementary information onto summary sheets. This would be followed by diagramming, charting, outlining and/or categorizing the information into tables. You can also write paragraph summaries of the information in your own words rather than simply reading the information from what you have created.

Another example of active study is to create summary sheets for a study session, main idea or concept. This will require you to read, write and think, thus making your study efforts more vigorous. Mapping is another active study method which requires a high level of critical thinking leading to greater comprehension of the material. This technique also helps to condense information into smaller, more manageable segments (see Appendix VIII).

No matter what method you choose or create, the important element is to be active. Use as many "bodily senses" as you can.

How can I make my studying more active?

Active study is far more beneficial than passive study. The active study format incorporates the use of some or all of your "bodily senses". For example, read aloud some information that you are having difficulty understanding or remembering. Continue by writing down, in your own words, what you just read. The retention of information increases as the use of your "bodily senses" increases for example, to both read and write the pertinent information.

How should I approach the reading content?

It is not necessary that everything be read (textbooks, outlines, old study notes etc.). What is necessary is making a study plan and sticking with it. When creating your study plan you want to keep in mind how much time you have for reading or re-reading information. In other words, you want to be selective about what you are going to spend time reading. Before you begin your readings, ask yourself the following questions.

- What do I want to gain from the reading?
- What are the important points that I am looking for in the reading?
- Have I structured the reading material into organized parts?

After a skimming of the readings, decide what parts are not necessary for your study session, what parts you merely need to review and what parts you need to emphasize. Once you have selected the information you have deemed important you should do the following:

- While you read the information write down key sentences or phrases and concentrate on understanding the ideas expressed.
- Read critically by asking yourself questions about the information regarding who, what, where, when and how.
- Recite the material to yourself immediately, testing yourself at the end of each part to enhance your recall for later.
- Read in any manner that is active.

Should I study in a group or alone?

Group study is also a form of active study. When you study in groups, others in the group might spot mistakes or point out things you've missed. The group can help to make up new questions you didn't think of and answer questions you didn't know. Further, the group forum can help to clarify uncertainties you may have.

Do I have an appropriate study environment?

Your study environment is a critical component of the study session. Always try to study using appropriate lighting conditions. If you can't study using natural light, then make sure your artificial light is as bright as possible. It can help to reduce the depression that studying for a test can sometimes cause. Try to minimize, as much as possible, distractions, including music. Conversely, fragrances can have an effect on you and can change your mood. If you wear a pleasant perfume or after shave lotion when you study or take a test, you may improve your chances of success.

What else should I know about my test preparations?

Do not get caught in the "studying what you already know trap". Identifying your strengths can be as important as identifying your weaknesses. If you have mastered certain information, move on and focus on what you don't know.

Taking simulated tests is an excellent tool for your study preparations. After taking the practice test, you must analyze your wrong answers. The analysis of your wrong answers should include the following.

- ❑ Take a careful look at the origin of the question (the textbooks, subdomains, supplemental material) to help steer you to the correct answer.
- ❑ Identify the reason you missed the question.
  - ○ Did you fail to read it correctly?
  - ○ Was the question at a higher cognitive level?
  - ○ Did you run out of time?
  - ○ Did the question cause a mental block?

This kind of analysis will help you avoid making the same errors of judgment on the certification examination.

Taking practice exams also helps sharpen your test taking speed. Many students fail the exam because they were unable to finish on time, leaving behind questions that could have been answered correctly, but weren't. Clearly, finishing the exam will increase your odds of successfully passing the exam. Allow yourself no more than a minute per question. In order to accomplish this, you must simulate the test taking environment. This requires an atmosphere that allows for no interruptions. Use a timer. This is a very integral portion of your test preparation. Practice taking an entire test under timed conditions.

What should I remember on exam day?

Address the least time consuming questions first. Your approach should be to answer the questions you do know and skip the ones you don't know. This will build your confidence for the questions that are more difficult and possibly cue you for the answers. Ration your time. Don't waste time on questions you don't fully understand. You can return to them later. Good luck!

10 RULES FOR EFFECTIVE STUDY

1 Start to study early----months before the exam.

2 Evaluate your strengths and weaknesses.

3 Study what you <u>don't know</u>, not what you do know.

4 Develop practical study strategies-- adopt an active study approach.

5 Be realistic when allocating your study time.

6 Construct a study schedule.

7 Be consistent with your study table and allow for deviations from your designated schedule.

8 Be creative with your study preparations. Utilize or design suitable study tools that enhance your efforts.

9 Form study groups.

10 You can't over-study—it is better to have studied too much than too little.

BILL OF RIGHTS FOR STUDY GROUPS

1. You have the right to limit group membership to no more than five and to dismiss members who consistently fail to meet their commitments as group members.

2. You have the right and responsibility to select study sites and times that are beneficial to all members.

3. You have a right to contribute to the formation of group goals which have measurable outcomes and deadlines.

4. You have the responsibility to be an active participant, not a passive receiver, in the group process. In addition, you have a right to expect active participation from other group members.

5. You have the right to have meetings begin and end promptly and to participate in study sessions without needless interruptions.

6. You have the right to participate in a group that is free from arguments and competition.

7. You have the right to expect that the group will stay on the task it sets for itself, and you have the responsibility for helping the group do so.

8. You have the right to take a break after an extended study session as long as the group resumes its study after the break.

9. You have the right to ask group members to limit socialization or discussion of extraneous topics to before and after study sessions.

10. You have the right to closure. This includes feelings of accomplishment.
    (1) At the end of each study session, evaluate to see if the group has met its goals.
    (2) After each exam, debrief members to evaluate test performances.
    (3) At the end of the group's duration, assess the value of the group experience to you.

Reference: Debbie G. Longman and Rhonda Atkinson, "Bill of Rights Promotes Study Groups" in August/September, 1992 *The Teaching Professor*, p. 5.

Section

3

CONTENT OUTLINES

Reviewing the content the fast way

It is safe to say that a review of several years of learning can not be accomplished in two to three months. So how can a compilation of several years worth of knowledge be approached?

An examination of the following content outlines is an easy way to review what you have learned and provides a means for assessing your strengths and weaknesses. A review of the outlines will stimulate your knowledge and help you to determine what content areas will require a more in-depth approach.

These outlines are presented as a basic overview to each of the health information content areas. They can be utilized not only as a "refresher" but as a study strategy. As each of the topics are carefully assessed, specific content areas that will require further consideration and attention can be identified. This will ensure that all essential information has been evaluated.

HEALTH RECORDS

THE RECORD

The health record is a compilation of pertinent facts of a patient's health history as well as sociological data. It includes the present and past illnesses and treatment. It is compiled by the individuals that contributed to the patient's care.

I. **Uses of the Health Record**
    A. Management of patient care
        1. follow the care and treatment of patient
    B. Quality Review
        1. evaluate the necessity, adequacy and appropriateness of care rendered
    C. Financial reimbursement
        1. substantiate the financial aspects of care rendered
    D. Legal Aspects
        1. protect legal interest of
            a. patient
            b. physician
            c. health care facility
    E. Education
        1. records can be used as case studies
    F. Research
        1. data contained in record can be used for research purposes
    G. Public Health
        1. identifies incidences of diseases

II. Health Record Flow

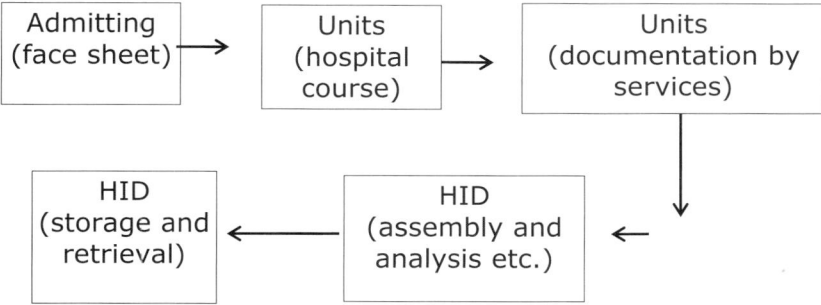

III. External Requirements for Health Records

A. Accreditation is a voluntary process that indicates the facility is operating based on specific, high standards.
   1. JCAHO
   2. CARF
   3. AOA
   4. ACS
   5. AAAHC
B. Licensure
   1. governmental activity
   2. gives legal approval for a facility to operate a specified number of beds or treat a specified number of patients
C. Medicare/Medicaid
   1. A facility must be certified to be reimbursed for services rendered to Medicare or Medicaid patients.
   2. JCAHO accreditation automatically certifies a facility for Medicare reimbursement.
   3. A facility must meet the Conditions of Participation (COP) if it is not accredited by JCAHO.

IV. Structure of Health Records

A. Order of the record
   1. chronological
   2. reverse chronological
B. Record formats
   1. Source oriented
      a. Reports are arranged in the record chronologically, by department from which they originated.
      b. Advantage: The reports from each source are organized together making it easier to determine the assessment, treatment and observations of that service.
      c. Disadvantage: It is not always possible to quickly determine all of the patient's problems and treatments at a given time since data from the various departments is organized in sections and not according to patient problem and/or not integrated in time sequence.
   2. Problem oriented (POMR)
      a. Each problem or condition of the patient is assigned a number.
      b. Each treatment and observation that is entered in the record is preceded by the appropriate problem number.
      c. Elements include:
         i. data base
         ii. problem list
         iii. initial plan
         iv. treatment/progress notes
      d. SOAP (subjective, objective, assessment and plan) is a format to document progress notes by all health care providers.
      e. Advantages
         i. One has the ability to see each problem individually with related problems.
         ii. It has a logical structure and a physician can easily assess and proceed with patient care and can follow one problem exclusively by following the number in the progress notes.
         iii. The reader can see the provider's approach in setting out the treatment plans.
      f. Disadvantage: The format requires additional training and commitment from medical and professional staff.

3. Integrated
    a. Reports are arranged in the patient's health record in strict chronological order regardless of the department of origin.
    b. Advantage: All information on a particular episode of care is together, giving a clear picture of patient's illness and response to treatment.
    c. Disadvantage: It is difficult to compare similar information over a period of time since all reports on one type are not together.
C. Differences in record keeping (content, documentation and formats)
    1. Acute care record
    2. Hospital-based ambulatory record
    3. ER record
    4. Free-standing ambulatory record
    5. Long term care record
    6. Home Care record
    7. Mental Health record
    8. Short-stay record (under 48 hours)
    9. Newborn record
    10. Hospice record

V. Health Record Analysis
A. Quantitative analysis identifies deficiencies in recording (omissions).
    1. review of specified areas of the medical record to identify deficiencies
        a. omissions (patient identification, reports, authentication of reports, proper documentation)
        b. each page of record identifies the patient
        c. content of record belongs in that record
        d. legibility (JCAHO recommends that when feasible, reports be typed)
        e. errors in documentation follow the appropriate guidelines:
            i. errors corrected by drawing a single line through mistake
            ii. write the word "error" near it
            iii. record the correct information
B. Qualitative analysis identifies inconsistencies and omissions that may indicate that the record is inaccurate or incomplete.
    1. protects legal interests
    2. meets external and internal requirements
    3. completes the record for final storage
    4. process
        a. check for complete and consistent recording of diagnostic statements
        b. check that entries are consistent
        c. check for appropriate description and justification for the hospital course
        d. check for appropriate and necessary informed consents
        e. check to ensure appropriate documentation
        f. check for any potential compensable events

C. Minimum Data Set
    1. purpose
    2. standard data items
        a. Uniform Hospital Discharge Data Set (UHDDS)
        b. Uniform Ambulatory Medical Care Minimum Data Set (UACDS)
        c. Minimum Data Set Long Term Care (MDS)
        d. Data Elements for Emergency Department Systems (DEEDS)
        e. Essential Medical Data Set (EMEDS)
        f. Health Plan Employer Data and Information Set (HEDIS)
        g. Outcomes and Assessment Information Set (OASIS)

RECORD CONTENT

I. Health Record Content
A. Face sheet
    1. basic patient information (i.e. demographics)
    2. admitting diagnoses
    3. final diagnoses without abbreviations or symbols
    4. operations performed
    5. consultant's name(s)
    6. disposition
    7. attending physician's signature
    8. consent for release of information
B. Discharge Summary

> *The Discharge Summary is a concise reason for hospitalization, findings, procedures performed, course of stay and condition on discharge.*

    1. Instructions must include diet, medication, activity and follow-up.
    2. All relevant diagnoses and operative procedures must be listed.
    3. Must have signature of authoring physician.
    4. A final note is acceptable if the patient was hospitalized for minor care less than 48 hours.
C. Emergency Room Record
    1. Must have documentation that patient was seen in the ER room.
    2. Documentation includes patient's problem, disposition of patient and is signed by physician.
D. Autopsy Report
    1. When an autopsy is performed, it is documented in physician's progress notes or nurse's notes.
    2. Provisional anatomic diagnoses must be present within 3 days of autopsy.
    3. The final autopsy report, signed by pathologist, must be part of chart within 60 days of autopsy.

E. History and Physical
   1. Components
      a. chief complaint
      b. present and past history
      c. review of systems
      d. immunization status
      e. allergies
      f. current medications
      g. physical exam
      h. impression
      i. plan of treatment
F. Physician Orders
   1. verbal and written
   2. must be dated and signed
   3. a discharge order must be written for each patient
   4. time frame for signatures and verbal orders must be documented in the Medical Staff Rules and Regulations
G. Progress Notes
   1. specific statement related to the course of a patient's illness, response to treatment, status at time of discharge.
   2. frequency must be documented by the Medical Staff rules and regulations
H. Consultation Report
   1. request by attending
   2. clinical opinion of a physician other than the attending
I. Operative Report
   1. is recorded for any patient who undergoes an invasive procedure
   2. includes
      a. pre-op diagnoses
      b. post-op diagnoses
      c. procedure performed
      d. surgeon and assistant(s)
      e. anesthesia
      f. description of findings
      g. description of operation
      h. specimens removed
      i. blood loss
      j. drains, packs, sponges
   3. should be dictated immediately following surgery
      a. If there is a transcription delay of up to 6 hours, a comprehensive progress note should be written immediately following surgery to maintain continuity of care.
J. Anesthesia Record
   1. includes:
      a. review of patient's history and physical
      b. pre-op medications
      c. anesthetic agent used
      d. patient's vital signs while under aesthetic
      e. patient's condition throughout the procedure
      f. pre-anesthesia note
      g. post-anesthesia note within 24 hours of anesthesia

K. Nurse's Notes
    1. must describe nursing diagnoses and patient's needs, nursing interventions and patient outcomes
    2. must
        a. be signed regarding admission/discharge of patient
        b. have a graphic chart of vital signs, pulse rate, respiration rate, blood pressure, intake/output, medications given and treatment given
    3. If the patient expires, a final note must include time patient pronounced dead; name of physician who made pronouncement; whether or not viable organ donation candidate; family notified or present; and disposition of body to morgue or funeral home.

L. Obstetric Record
    1. includes
        a. antepartum that was started in physician's office
        b. labor record
        c. delivery record
        d. postpartum record

M. Newborn Record
    1. includes
        a. birth history
        b. NB identification form, which includes mother's MR admission number, NB sex, date/time of birth, weight, length, foot/finger prints
        c. NB physical exam

N. Transfer Form
    1. must accompany patient if transferred to another facility
    2. include
        a. accepting physician's name
        b. reason for transfer
        c. medications given
        d. testing done
        e. signed by nurse

O. Discharge Instructions
    1. should be written in a way that the patient can understand
    2. include
        a. activity
        b. dietary restrictions
        c. medications to be taken including dose and frequency
        d. what medication is for
        e. signatures of physician and patient/guardian to indicate patient understands

DOCUMENTATION ISSUES

I. Appropriate Documentation
  A. Determined by
    1. hospital and medical staff policies
    2. Medicare's Condition's of Participation
    3. Accreditation Organizations
    4. licensure requirements
  B. Documentation of signatures
    1. JCAHO requires entries be dated
    2. JCAHO requires a method of identifying authors of entries
    3. signature stamps are allowed by JCAHO if there is a signed statement in physician's credential file and the HIM department stating that only the individual whose signature is represented will use it
  C. Abbreviations and symbols
    1. used only when they have been approved by medical staff and they can only have one meaning
  D. Timeliness
    1. made as close as possible to the time of the occurrence of the events
    2. JCAHO requires completion within 30 days of discharge
  E. Legibility
    1. JCAHO recommends that reports be typed when possible
  F. Corrections
    1. errors should be corrected by drawing a single line through mistake
    2. write an explanation of mistake near it
    3. time/date and record correct information
    4. no erasures should be made ever
    5. late entries should be marked as a late entry with an explanation as to why the documentation is out of sequence

ISSUES AFFECTED BY THE RECORD

I. Incomplete Record Control

> *Incomplete records are records with specific deficiencies that have been identified through qualitative or quantitative analysis, that can be completed by the health care provider. The provider is required to complete any unfinished documentation within a specified period of time as stated in the medical staff rules and regulations of the Medical Staff By-Laws.*

A. Incomplete record definition
   1. Incomplete record rate

RATE:

$$\frac{\text{\# of incomplete medical records}}{\text{\# of discharges during required completion period}}$$

   2. Filing incomplete records
      a. May be filed in permanent file to save on retrieval time, but the records are less assessable to the providers.
      b. May be filed in a separate file by provider name. They are most assessable to providers this way but it requires a cross reference system.
      c. May be filed in a separate file by medical record number (combination).
      d. If record remains incomplete after the death of a provider, facility policy should be followed for filing incomplete records in the permanent file.
   3. Final chart check or re-analysis
   4. File in permanent file
   5. Incomplete filing policies should be written and distributed to the appropriate individuals.

B. Delinquent record

> *A delinquent medical record is a record that has not been completed within the specified period, as stated the Medical Staff By-Laws, following the patient's discharge.*

DELINQUENT RATE:

$$\frac{\text{Delinquent medical records}}{\text{average \# of discharges during a completion period}}$$

Note: Go to the JCAHO web site at: JCAHO.org. In the "search" section type in "delinquency" and you will see a link for the 2004 Hospital Medical Record Statistics Form which determines compliance with IM.6.10 EP10.

C. JCAHO requirements
  1. The time period is to be specified in medical staff by-laws and never to exceed 30 days.
  2. Consequences of delinquent records
     a. Type 1 recommendation is attached to the accreditation decision if
        i. the total number of medical records delinquent for any reason exceeds 50 percent of the average monthly discharges
        ii. the number of medical records delinquent due to the absence of a medical H&P exceeds 9 records or 2 percent of the average monthly discharges whichever is greater
        iii. the number of medical records delinquent due to the absence of an operative report exceeds 9 records or 2% of the average monthly operative procedures whichever is greater
  3. Delinquent and/or Incomplete Record Reports should be submitted to the Credential Committee and other Peer Review and Re-appointment Committees
  4. Record is completed when
     a. required contents (e.g. discharge summary, final progress note etc.) are assembled and authenticated
     b. all final diagnoses and any complications are recorded without the use of symbols and abbreviations
  5. Computerized incomplete systems are available and can
     a. generate printed lists of incomplete records
     b. generate notices to the provider whose records are delinquent
     c. generate a list of deficiencies for the department chairpersons
     d. compute statistics
     e. track location of incomplete records

INFORMATION REQUIRED FROM THE RECORD

I. Indexes and Registers
  A. MPI
     1. contents
        a. varies according to needs of facility and regulatory agencies
     2. filing rules
        a. must be specific
     3. methods of filing
        a. alphabetical
        b. phonetic
           i. initial of surname by sound for rest of name
     4. numerical
     5. equipment and supplies (manual)
        a. index cards if manual system is used
           i. 3x5; 100 cards/inch; average weight stock
        b. index guides
           i. extend 3/8 of an inch
        c. filing equipment
           i. 500,000 cards use elevator file
     6. control for index
        a. access to index
        b. preparation of index cards
        c. security and separate files

B. Number index (see Retention/Retrieval Outline)
  1. content of the number file
  2. sources of the index
  3. maintaining the number index
C. Disease and Operations index
  1. should provide sufficient information required for medical and statistical reports and requests
  2. JCAHO, Medicare/Medicaid require data for surveys
  3. data typically collected includes
     a. patient's sex, age, race/ethnicity
     b. attending physician
     c. code for service area
     d. discharge disposition
     e. admit and discharge date
     f. length of stay
     g. charges and costs
     h. associated diseases and procedure codes
  4. should be maintained for at least 10 years
  5. indexing and cross-indexing of diseases and operation codes
  6. group indexing of disease and operation codes
  7. Uses may include
     a. review of previous cases of given disease in order to manage current patient's health problem
     b. testing of theories and comparison of data
     c. evaluate quality of patient care
     d. to accumulate risk management data
     e. provide data for licensing and surveys
D. Computerized Disease and Operation Indexes
  1. in-house computer or commercial discharge data service
  2. compare cost of in-house vs. commercial service
E. Physician index
  1. provides each medical personnel with record of patients treated
  2. entries include
     a. patient's name, medical record number
     b. hospital service
     c. length of stay
     d. charges and costs
F. Registers (contain more data than indexes; all have processes for case definition, case finding and data collection)
  1. Disease Registry
     a. secondary data related to patients with specific diagnosis, condition or procedure
  2. Trauma Registry
  3. Birth defects Registry
  4. Diabetes Registry
  5. Implant Registry
  6. Transplant Registry
  7. Immunization Registry
  8. Cancer Registry

II. Cancer Program
A. Four Components of a Cancer Program approved Commission on Cancer of ACS
   1. multidisciplinary cancer committee
   2. multidisciplinary cancer conferences
   3. quality outcome and improvement
   4. cancer registry

Established for the collection and maintenance of comprehensive patient care data on all cancer patients. Its objective is to provide lifetime follow-up of cancer patients and to provide meaningful information to physicians for patient care evaluation and research. There are three (3) types of registries.
1. *Hospital based, which operates exclusively for cancer patients treated at a particular facility.*
2. *The second type is a central registry. This can be either a population-based or the main registry for a group of hospital-based registries. It collects data from its designated territory, thus accumulating enough information to study trends in cancer occurrence, treatments and results.*
3. *The third type is a special-purpose registry. It collects data on one type of cancer, such as breast cancer, lung cancer, colon cancer etc. The purpose of all of these is to improve the treatment and management of cancer, now and in the future.*

B. ACS guidelines address the following criteria
   1. reference date
   2. case eligibility
   3. patient eligibility
   4. patient index
   5. case-finding
   6. accession registry
      a. chronological listing of all patients
   7. accession registry
   8. abstracting
   9. coding
   10. staging
   11. primary site file
   12. quality control
C. Patient Follow-up
   1. follow-up file
   2. follow-up forms and letters

References for Health Records

Health Information Management of a Strategic Resource, 2nd Edition
Abdelhak, et. al.
W. B. Saunders, 2001

Health Information Management Technology
Johns, Merida
AHIMA, 2002

Health Information Management
LaTour and Eichenwald
AHIMA, 2003

HEALTH INFORMATION RETENTION AND RETRIEVAL

FILING SYSTEMS

I. Record Numbering and Filing Systems

The filing system is a result of the numbering system for unit and serial record keeping. You should be able to describe and give advantages and disadvantages of each system.

- A. Fundamentals
    1. ensure safety of the record
    2. types of retrieval systems
- B. Numbering systems
    1. serial
    2. unit-preferred by JCAHO
    3. serial-unit
    4. other adaptations
        a. social security
        b. family
- C. Filing Systems
    1. straight numeric
        a. chronological order
        b. easy to train personnel
        c. harder to detect misfiles
        d. transposition of numbers
        e. heavy filing in one area
        f. quality control is difficult
    2. terminal digit
        a. 100 primary sections from 00-99
        b. may be referred to as 2-2-2 filing
        c. unusually six (6) part number, hyphenated
        d. 100 primary sections
        e. second tertiary digit is changing
        f. records are equally distributed
        g. work assignments can be divided
        h. misfiles reduced
        i. can use pre-printed color-coded folders
        j. training of personnel longer
    3. middle digit
        a. similar to terminal digit
        b. primary digit in middle position
        c. disadvantage due to long training time
        d. gaps in the files when records are pulled and difficulty with longer numbers
    4. Alphabetical
    5. Alphanumeric
- D. Converting to terminal/middle digit filing
    1. start at beginning of year or when moving to new area
    2. convert old files as patients are readmitted
    3. prepare new area with section guides
    4. sort records by primary digits
    5. find misfiles
    6. account for all numbers

II. File Expansion
  A. Affected by numbering system
      1. Unit: leave 25% of the shelves open for expansion purposes
  B. Purging
      1. easy with serial and serial-unit numbering and filing (lower numbers are old admission)
      2. unit system requires individual inspection (may use yearly color-coded tabs)
  C. Number Sources
      1. facility decides
      2. a longer number can be divided into segments with middle or terminal digit filing
      3. numbers may be issued from HID or patient registration
  D. Changing system
      1. from serial to unit
          a. set a date
          b. assign readmitted patients a new unit number
          c. bring old records forward
      2. leave cross reference in file
      3. leave records of patients not readmitted in original file until purging
  E. Converting to terminal/middle digit filing
      1. start at beginning of year or when moving to new area
      2. convert old files as patients are readmitted
      3. prepare new area with section guides
      4. sort records by primary digits
      5. find misfiles
      6. account for all numbers

III. Storage Systems
  A. Shelving (vertical, lateral open, compressed)
      1. vertical open shelf
          a. advantages/disadvantages
      2. lateral cabinet
      3. compressed (used only with small staff)
          a. mobile
          b. lateral mobile
      4. other considerations
          a. 36 inches recommended for aisles between units (30-inch minimum)
          b. 5 feet for opening with face-to-face drawer cabinets
      5. Process for purchasing units
          a. determine both linear filing inches provided by the units and the number of filing inches currently used plus expansion (inches per shelf x shelves per unit = filing inches)
          b. for unit record, leave 25 percent of shelf open for expansion
          c. inches per shelf times number of shelves in each unit = linear filing inches in each unit
          d. once filing inches are determined, shelving units can be calculated (filing inches divided by filing inches per units)

```
┌──────────────────────────────────────────────────────────────────┐
│                            Example                                 │
│  A HID currently utilizes 10 units, 6 shelves high to store        │
│  records.                                                          │
│  How many linear filing inches are in each unit?                   │
│  33" per shelf x 6 shelves = 198 filing inches in each unit        │
│                                                                    │
│  Presently 1705 filing inches are required to store the records.   │
│  An additional 500 filing inches are necessary to allow for        │
│  expansion.                                                        │
│  How many units need to be purchased?                              │
│  500 divided by 198 = 3 units                                      │
│                                                                    │
│    If the units exceed the whole number, round up to the next      │
│  whole number.                                                     │
│  (Remember, you can't purchase a part of a unit – you must         │
│  purchase a whole unit.)                                           │
└──────────────────────────────────────────────────────────────────┘
```

IV. Image and Electronic Storage
  - A. Microfilm
    1. roll
    2. jacket microfiche
    3. microfiche
  - B. Image based
    1. document canning
  - C. Considerations
    1. legal considerations for micrographics
    2. cost of micrographics
    3. contracted microfilm service bureaus

V. Retrieval and Tracking Systems
  - A. Guides
    1. assist in expediting the filing and finding of records
    2. more guides needed for thick records
    3. consider durability and visibility of guides when purchasing
    4. formulas

```
┌──────────────────────────────────────────────────────────────────┐
│        FORMULA: To Determine the Number of Guides Needed           │
│                                                                    │
│     total number of records                                        │
│  number of records between guides    = total # of guides needed    │
│                                                                    │
│  If total number of records is unknown, multiply the filing        │
│  inches by the average number of records per inch                  │
│                                                                    │
│  total number of guides needed                                     │
│        primary sections           = guides in each primary section │
└──────────────────────────────────────────────────────────────────┘
```

  5. terminal guides are permanent whereas serial or middle guides must be changed
  6. terminal digit and middle digit: two pairs of numbers appear on the guide:
     <u>00</u> secondary
     65 primary
     - a. in a terminal digit file, the first record behind guide 00 would be 00-00-65, followed by 01-00-65

7. determine the numbering pattern on guides (terminal digit)

FORMULA:
To Determine the Number of Guides Within Each Primary Section

$$\frac{\text{total number of guides}}{100(\# \text{ of primary sections})} = \# \text{ of guides within each primary section}$$

---

    a. once the number of guides within each primary section has been determined, divide the number of guides by 100 to establish the number pattern

---

Example: To Determine Number Pattern
    5000 total guides needed
    5000 divided by 100 primary sections
    = 50 guides in each section

100 primary divided by 50 guides in each section **= 2**

pattern on guides: 00-00
                                02-00
                                04-00

VI. Other Record Filing Considerations
  A. Record folders
    1. file folders are scored or bellowed
    2. can be pre-printed, with year printed for ease in purging
    3. color coding
      a. use to prevent misfiles
      b. more effective with middle and terminal digit filing systems
      c. limit colors to 2 or 3
  B. Record control systems
    1. requisitions
      a. completed by requester
      b. specify time for delivery
    2. charge-out system
      a. always replace record with an outguide and requisition slip
      b. return policies should be in place
    3. out-guides
  C. Automated chart location system
    1. tracks record location using computer (i.e. bar code)
    2. recommended for high record activity
  D. Misfiles
    1. transposition of digits
    2. check hundreds group preceding of following
    3. check file before and after
  E. Organization of files
    1. centralized
      a. advantages and disadvantages
    2. decentralized
      a. advantages and disadvantages

OTHER RETENTION AND RETRIEVAL ISSUES

I. **MPI (key to locating patient record)**
   A. Identifies all patients
      1. maintenance (manual or computerized)
      2. maintained permanently
      3. by alphabet
      4. by soundex
   B. Content
   C. Security and Retention Issues

II. **Automated Record Tracking Systems**
   A. Software considerations
      1. features
      2. requirements
   B. Data entry capabilities
   C. Hardware needs

III. **Record Retention and Destruction**
   A. Written policy needed
   B. Consider
      1. readmission rate
      2. research
      3. statute of limitations
      4. cost of microfilming
      5. licensure requirements
      6. Medicare requirements
      7. what to retain
   C. Inactive records
      1. storage
         a. commercial
         b. in-house
   D. Facility Closures
      1. Issues to consider
   E. Microfilming
      1. advantages and disadvantages
      2. types
      3. in-house or off site
      4. considerations
      5. equipment needs (reader/printer)
      6. microfilming process

IV. **Quality Controls**
   A. Establish measures
      1. accuracy of filing record (standards and rates)
      2. filing volume (standards and rates)
      3. filing of loose material (standards and rates)
   B. Establish monitoring system

References for Health Records Retention and Retrieval

HIM Textbooks

Introduction to Health Information Technology
   Davis, N. and LaCour, M. (2002). W. B. Saunders

Health Information Management
   Huffman, E., (1994). Physician Record Services

Health Information Management Technology: An Applied Approach
   Johns, Merida, (2002). AHIMA

Health Information Management: Concepts, Principles and Practice
   LaTour, K., and Eichenwald, K (2002). AHIMA

Health Information Management: Principles and Organization for Health Information Services
   Skurka, M. (2003). Jossey-Bass

Organization Manuals

Joint Commission on Accreditation of Healthcare Organizations
   Accreditation Manual for Hospital, Management of Information Standard IM7.9

American College of Surgeons
   Cancer Program Manual

AHIMA PRACTICE BRIEFS

AHIMA Practice Brief: "Managing Multimedia Medical Records: A Health Information Manager's Role"
AHIMA Practice Brief: "Information Security: A Checklist for Healthcare Professionals"
AHIMA Practice Brief: "Developing Information Capture Tools"
AHIMA Practice Brief: "Protecting Patient Information After A Facility Closure"
AHIMA Practice Brief: "Disaster Planning for Health Information (Updated)"
AHIMA Practice Brief: "Master Patient (Person) Index (MPI) – Recommended Core Data Elements"
AHIMA Practice Brief: "Retention of Health Information"
AHIMA Practice Brief: "Destruction of Patient Health Information"
AHIMA Practice Brief: "Merging Master Patient (Person) Indexes"

FORMS

I. Information Captured
    A. What is the best means of efficiently capturing information?
        1. it is the information that must be considered not the form or the computer screen
        2. paper and screens are only the tools
    B. Creation of form
        1. define the purpose and identify users
        2. meet the needs of the end user
        3. easy to use
        4. ensure there are no duplications

II. Objectives of Information Capture Control
    A. Maximize efficiency through effective design of forms and computer screens
    B. Establish and control standards for information capture and usage
    C. Originate and maintain proper specifications for information capture and usage
    D. Ensure consistent, accurate capture of information
    E. Streamline the information capture process
        1. eliminate duplicate data entry
        2. ensure that information capture follows the flow of the work
        3. reduce key strokes
        4. ensure that users have the information when needed

III. Forms Committee
    A. Structure
        1. develop, review and control all organizational information capture tools
        2. composed of information users and gatherers
    B. Membership
        1. HIM personnel
        2. medical staff
        3. nursing staff
        4. purchasing
        5. information systems
        6. Quality Improvement personnel
        7. forms vendor representative
    C. Responsibilities
        1. review and approve all printed material
        2. ensure that forms used are standardized in an acceptable format
        3. establish a listing of all approved forms
        4. review all printed material for the organizational name, logo, address, form number and date of revision
        5. review forms used consistently and regularly
        6. consult with appropriate departments when a request for new form(s) is/are made

IV. Principles of Forms Design

A. Consider the following when designing a paper form
1. forms numbering system
2. study the purpose and use of the form and design it with the user's needs
3. keep design simple
4. include title, form number, date of creation or revision, logo and organization's name and address
5. include signature lines when appropriate
6. use standardized terminology
7. if using multi-part paper, list distribution of copies
8. arrange items on forms in proper sequence
9. allow for sufficient spacing for the method of fill in: manual or machine
10. appropriate patient identifying information
11. optical reader codes and bar codes should be printed in the upper left hand corner of form
12. consider copying needs of form in terms of size
13. because of faxing, copying and imaging, the best form colors are black ink on white paper
14. allow 3/4 inch margin for documents that will require hole punching
15. margins should be at least 3/8 inch wide
16. paper ranging from 20-24 pounds in weight is recommended for use in copiers, scanners and fax machines
17. normal font size need not be limited to 12 points, although avoid use of a type point smaller than 9 points for lower case and 10 points for upper case letters

B. Additional considerations
1. paper stock and ink
2. paper size
3. paper color
4. typeface
5. special effects
6. multipart forms
7. hole punches
8. margins
9. headers
10. color coding

V. Forms Control, Tracking and Management

A. Written policies and guidelines
B. Develop a system to identify all forms
C. New forms should follow a pilot program before final approval
D. Creation of a quality control mechanism
E. Proper storage of forms

VI. Form Analysis

A. Initiating forms/re-evaluating forms
1. need
   a. why this need
      i. what justifies the form's existence
      ii. what other forms are related or duplicated
      iii. what inadequacies are there in the forms
2. people
   a. why by these people
      i. who requires the data
      ii. who enters the information
      iii. who extracts the information
3. place
   a. why here
      i. where are the forms written and processed
      ii. where are the forms sent
      iii. where are the forms filed
4. time
   a. why at this time
      i. when are the forms written
      ii. when are the forms processed
      iii. when are the forms filed
5. method
   a. why this method
      i. how are the forms written
      ii. how is the information in the forms processed
      iii. how are the forms transmitted
      iv. how are the forms filed

VII. Elements of Computer View Design

A. users
1. limit view and access to minimum necessary
2. users should be allowed to retrieve and enter information in the way they desire
3. reduce the number of keystrokes
4. the computer fields should follow an appropriate sequence
5. use pop up menus where appropriate and needed
6. information should be entered only once and then shared
7. determine the correct size of the document (not too much or too little information per screen)
8. use eye catching features (color, fonts, and flashing characters) to enhance the communication
9. use standardized vocabularies

References for Forms

Health Information Management of a Strategic Resource, 2nd Edition
  Abdelhak, et. Al.
  W. B. Saunders, 2001

Health Information Management Technology
  Johns, Merida
  AHIMA, 2002

Health Information Management
  LaTour and Eichenwald
  AHIMA, 2003

CLASSIFICATION SYSTEMS AND NOMENCLATURES

I. Definitions
A. Classification Systems – Systems that group related entities to produce statistical information.
B. Nomenclatures – Systems of names in any science or art.
C. Clinical Terminologies – Standardized terms and their synonyms that can be mapped to broader classifications.

II. Current Coding Systems
A. International Classification of Diseases, Ninth Edition, Clinical Modification (ICD-9-CM)
    1. Volumes 1 and 2 – Diagnosis codes (example: 250.00)
    2. Volume 3 – Codes for hospital inpatient procedures (example: 51.23)
    3. ICD-9 developed by WHO
    4. ICD-9-CM diagnostic codes maintained by National Center for Health Statistics (NCHS)
    5. ICD-9-CM procedure codes maintained by Centers for Medicare and Medicaid Services (CMS)
    6. Annual modifications are implemented on October 1 of each year.
B. International Classification of Diseases, Tenth Revision, Clinical Modification (ICD-10-CM)
    1. Alphanumeric six-digit codes
    2. Greater specificity in code assignments
    3. Alphabetic Index and Tabular List
    4. Based on ICD-10 developed by WHO. Modification by NCHS
C. International Classification of Diseases, Tenth Revision, Procedural Coding System (ICD-10-PCS)
    1. Developed by 3M Health Information Systems for CMS
    2. Seven-digit alphanumeric codes
        a. completeness
        b. expandability
        c. standardized terminology
        d. multiaxial structure
D. CPT (Nomenclature and Classification)
    1. Codes for physicians' procedures and services (example: 32016)
    2. Developed and maintained by the American Medical Association
    3. Annual modifications are implemented on January 1 of each year.
    4. CPT-5 Introduces three new categories of codes
        a. Category I codes: 5-digit codes as in CPT-4
        b. Category II codes: Optional tracking codes used in performance measurement
        c. Category III codes: Temporary codes for new and emerging procedures and services
E. HCPCS
    1. Level I
        a. Five-digit CPT codes (example: 10530)
    2. Level II
        a. Alphanumeric national codes (example: J0320)
        b. Developed and maintained by CMS
    3. Level III
        a. Alphanumeric local codes (example: W0002)
        b. Discontinued by CMS Jan 1, 2004

F. United Medical Language System Metathesaurus (UMLS)
   1. National Library of Medicine (NLM) project began in 1986 and is ongoing
   2. Purpose is to aid in development of systems to retrieve and integrate electronic biomedical information from a variety of sources
G. Diagnostic and Statistical Manual (DSM-IV)
   1. Developed and maintained by the American Psychiatric Association (APA)
   2. Provides codes and diagnostic criteria for mental disorders
H. International Classification of Diseases—Oncology (ICD-O)
   1. Developed and maintained by the World Health Organization (WHO)
   2. Provides codes for classifying neoplasms according to site, behavior and morphology
I. Systemized Nomenclature of Human and Veterinary Medicine (SNOMED)
   1. Developed and maintained by the American College of Pathologists (CAP)
   2. Provides codes for a variety of information found throughout the medical record such as diagnoses, signs and symptoms and procedures
J. Systemized Nomenclature of Medicine Reference Terminology (SNOMED-RT)
   1. Concept-based terminology (110,000 concepts with linkages to 180,000 terms)
   2. Concepts presented in tables
   3. Relationships presented in tables
K. Read Codes
   1. Developed by Computer Aided Medical Systems Limited in the United Kingdom
   2. Provides a list of terms to describe care for use in computerized formats
L. Logical Observation Identifier Names and Codes (LOINC)
   1. Provides a method of standardizing terminology and codes for identifying individual laboratory results, clinical observations and diagnostic study evaluations
M. International Classification for Primary Care (ICPC-2)
   1. Developed by World Organization of Family Doctors (WONCA) International Classification Committee (WICC) Merger of
      a. Reason for Encounter Classification (RFEC)
      b. International Classification of Process in Primary Care (IC-Process-PC)
      c. International Classification of Health Problems in Primary Care, Second Edition, Defined (ICHPPC-2D)
      d. Mapped to ICD-10
N. Nursing Classification Systems
   1. North American Nursing Diagnosis Association (NANDA)
   2. Nursing Interventions Classifications (NIC)
   3. Nursing Outcomes Classification (NOC)
   4. Omaha System
   5. Home Health Care Classification (HHCC)
   6. Patient Care Data Set (PCDS)
   7. Nursing Management Minimum Data Set (NMMDS)
   8. Perioperative Nursing Dataset
   9. SNOMED-RT
   10. Nursing Minimum Data Sets (NMDS)
   11. International Classification for Nursing Practice (ICNP)
   12. ABC codes

O. Medical Dictionary for Drug Regulatory Affairs (MedDRA)
   1. Standardized medical terminology developed for regulation of pharmaceutical industry
   2. International reporting of adverse drug reactions
P. International Classification of Functioning, Disability and Health (ICIDH-2)
   1. Developed by the World Health Organization (WHO)
   2. Classifies disabilities by body function and structure, by activities and participation and by environmental factors

III. Historical Coding Systems
A. Standard Nomenclature of Diseases and Operations (SNDO)
   1. Published by the AMA
   2. Dual classification using site and etiology as disease axis and site and procedure as procedure axis (example: 600-392)
B. Current Medical Information and Terminology (CMIT)
   1. Published by the AMA
   2. Nomenclature
C. The International Classification of Diseases, Adapted for Use in the United States, Eighth Edition (ICDA-8) preceded ICD-9-CM
D. The Hospital Adaptation of ICDA (H-ICDA)
   1. Published by the Commission on Professional and Hospital Activities

References for Classification Systems and Nomenclatures

Health Information: Management of a Strategic Resource 2nd Edition
   Abdelhak, Mervat; Grostick, Sara; Hanken, Mary Alice; Jacobs, Ellen
   W. B. Saunders. Philadelphia, PA., 2001

ICD-9-CM Coding Handbook for 2004
   Brown, Faye
   American Hospital Association. Chicago, IL. 2003

Step-by-Step Medical Coding 4th Edition
   Buck, Carol J.
   W. B. Saunders. Philadelphia, PA., 2002

Coding Clinic
   American Hospital Association. Chicago, IL.

ICD-9-CM Diagnostic Coding and Reimbursement for Physician Services 2004
   Hazelwood, Anita C. and Venable, Carol A.
   American Health Information Management Association. Chicago, IL. 2003

ICD-9-CM Code Book with October 2003 updates
   Channel Publishing, Ltd.
   INGENIX

Health Information Management Technology An Applied Approach
   Johns, Merida.
   American Health Information Management Association. Chicago, IL, 2002

Health Information Management: Concepts, Principles and Practice
   LaTour, Kathleen and Eichenwald, Shirley
   American Health Information Management Association. Chicago, IL. 2002

Physicians' Current Procedural Terminology: CPT 2004, Professional Edition.
   American Medical Association. Chicago, IL. 2003

Principles of CPT Coding.
   American Medical Association. Chicago, IL. 2003

Effective Management of Coding Services
   Schraffenberger, Lou Ann
   American Health Information Management Association. Chicago, IL. 2002

Basic ICD-9-CM Coding
   Schraffenberger, Lou Ann
   American Health Information Management Association. Chicago, IL, 2003

Basic CPT/HCPCS Coding 2003
   Smith, Gail.
   American Health Information Management Association. Chicago, IL, 2003

REIMBURSEMENT

I. **Fee-For-Service**
   A. Patient pays provider after service is rendered

II. **Commercial Insurance**
   A. Private Insurance
      1. Payment of premiums to cover individuals or families
      2. Insurance policies spell out
         a. medical services covered
         b. when the company will pay for services
         c. how much and for long the company will pay for covered services
         d. how claims will be submitted
   B. Employer-Based Self-Insurance Plans
      1. Employer pays insurance claims for employees

III. **Blue Cross and Blue Shield Plans**
   B. 48 independent, locally operated companies
   C. Insures
      1. individuals
      2. small businesses
      3. seniors
      4. large employer groups

IV. **Government-Sponsored Healthcare Programs**
   A. Medicare
      1. Pays for healthcare services provided to
         a. Social Security beneficiaries
         b. permanently disabled
         c. certain other groups
      2. Part A
         a. Pays for
            i. inpatient care
            ii. long-term care
            iii. SNF
            iv. home health care
            v. hospice care
         b. Free to individuals 65 years of age and older and eligible for Social Security or Railroad Retirement benefits
      3. Part B
         a. Pays for:
            i. outpatient care
            ii. physician services
            iii. other practitioner's services
         b. Fee deducted from social security checks
      4. Part C
         a. Medicare + Choice
         b. The following types of plans are included
            i. Coordinated care plans including health maintenance organizations
            ii. Private, unrestricted, fee-for-service plans
            iii. Medical savings account (MSA) plans

B. Medicaid
    1. Title XIX Social Security Act
    2. Medical care for low income families
    3. Cooperative with states
C. TRICARE
    1. Healthcare program for active-duty members of military and family
D. The Civilian Health and Medical Program-Veterans Administration (CHAMPVA)
    1. Provides health care to
        a. dependents and survivors of permanently and totally disabled veterans
        b. survivors of veterans who died from service-related conditions
        c. survivors of military personnel who died in line of duty
E. Indian Health Service
F. Workers' Compensation
    1. Federal
    2. State

V. Managed Care
A. Prepaid health plans that integrate financial and delivery aspects of healthcare services
B. National Committee for Quality Assurance (NCQA) accredits, assesses and reports on the quality of managed care plans in US
C. Health Plan Employer Data and Information Set (HEDIS) used by NCQA
D. Types of Managed Care Plans
    1. Health maintenance organizations (HMOs)
    2. Preferred provider organizations (PPOs)
    3. Point-of-service (POS) plans
    4. Exclusive provider organizations (EPOs)
    5. Integrated delivery systems (IDSs)

VI. Healthcare Reimbursement Methodologies
A. Fee-for-service
    1. Chargemaster
    2. Based on usual, customary and reasonable charges
B. Managed fee-for-service
    1. Managed care plans control costs by managing member's use of healthcare services
    2. Prospective and retrospective utilization review
    3. Discharge planning as utilization control
C. Global Payment
    1. Single payment covers planning and completing a procedure

D. Prospective Payment Plans
1. Diagnosis Related Groups (DRGs)
   a. Classification based on resource utilization
   b. Inpatient care for Medicare patients
   c. DRGs assigned by Grouper
   d. ICD-9-CM diagnosis and procedure codes divided into
      i. Major Diagnostic Categories (MDCs)
      ii. Medical Subdivision
      iii. Surgical Subdivision
      iv. Principal Diagnosis
      v. Complications
      vi. Comorbidities
   e. Each patient assigned to one DRG
   f. Payment according to DRG
      i. DRG weight X hospital rate = Payment
      ii. Case Mix – Average of DRG weights
   g. Coding for inpatient prospective payment
      i. Care in selection of principal diagnosis
      ii. Review of entire medical record necessary
      iii. Coding quality
         • monitoring
         • auditing
         • Medicare code editor
         • coding compliance programs
      iv. Claims submitted
         • on UB-92 form
         • to fiscal intermediary
2. Resource-Based Relative Value Scale (RBRVS) System
   a. Physicians services
   b. Based on
      i. Relative value units for physician work
      ii. Practice expenses
      iii. Malpractice costs
      iv. Payment localities adjusted to geographic practice cost indices
      v. National conversion factor
3. Medicare Skilled Nursing Facility Prospective Payment System (SNF PPS)
   a. Covers all costs to Medicare Part A beneficiaries
   b. Per diem prospective system based on case-mix adjustment payment rates
   c. Resource Utilization Groups Version III (RUG-III)
      i. Uses resident assessment date from the Minimum Data Set 2.0 (MDS) to assign patients to one of forty-four groups
4. Resident Assessment Validation and Entry (RAVEN)
   a. computerized data entry system for long-term care facilities
   b. ICD-9-CM codes used for diagnosis and procedure reporting for Part A patients
   c. ICD-9-CM diagnostic codes and HCPCS procedure codes are reported for Part B patients

5. Medicare/Medicaid Outpatient Prospective Payment System (OPPS)
   a. Includes the following services
      i. hospital outpatient services
      ii. partial hospitalization services
      iii. partial hospitalization services provided by community mental health centers (CMHCs)
      iv. Vaccines, splints, casts and antigens for home health
      v. Vaccines provided by comprehensive outpatient rehabilitation facilities (CORFs)
      vi. Splints, casts and antigens provided to hospice patients for treatment of non-terminal illnesses
   b. Calculation of payment based on Ambulatory Payment Classification (APCs)
      i. More than 450 APCs
      ii. Services within APC are similar clinically and use of resources
      iii. Each APC is assigned a fixed payment rate
      iv. Payment rates adjusted according to hospital wage index
      v. Payment status indicators
      vi. Packaging
      vii. Discounting
      viii. More than one APC may be assigned to a patient
   c. Coding Systems for OPPS
      i. Diagnoses are coded with ICD-9-CM
      ii. Procedures are coded with HCPCS
   d. Claim Submission
      i. Claims submitted on CMS-1500 form for non-hospital patients
      ii. Claims submitted on UB-92 form for hospital outpatients
6. Medicare Ambulatory Surgery Centers
   a. Non-hospital surgery center certified by Medicare
   b. Ambulatory Surgery Center (ASC) rates
      i. Procedures divided into 8 categories with payment for each category
      ii. Payment for more than one procedure during single operative session
         - 100% of rate for one procedure
         - 50% of rate for second procedure
         - 25% of rate for additional procedures
7. Home Health Prospective Payment System (HH PPS)
   a. Case-mix system- home health resources groups (HHRGs)
   b. Data for HH PPS
      i. outcomes and assessment information set (OASIS)
      ii. groups cases to appropriate HHRG (C0F0S0)
   c. HIPPS codes on claims
      i. five-position alphanumeric codes representing patient characteristics (HAEJ1)
8. Inpatient Rehabilitation Facility Prospective Payment System (IRF PPS)
   a. Patient assessment instrument used to classify patients into case-mix groups (CMGs)
   b. ICD-9-CM codes in IRF patient assessment instrument
   c. Determination of CMG depends upon
      i. rehabilitation impairment codes (RIC)
      ii. motor admission score
      iii. cognitive admission score
      iv. age
      v. medical complications

Abdelhak, Mervat; Grostick, Sara; Hanken, Mary Alice; Jacobs, Ellen, *Health Information: Management of a Strategic Resource*, 2nd Edition
W. B. Saunders, Philadelphia, PA, 2001.

Federal Register, Department of Health and Human Services-Center for Medicare and Medicaid Services. Vol. 65 No. 68. Medicare Program, "*Prospective Payment System for Hospital Outpatient Services; Final Rule.*" Friday, April 7, 2000.

Federal Register. Department of Health and Human Services-Center for Medicare and Medicaid Services. Vol. 66 No. 148. Medicare Program, "*Changes to the Hospital Inpatient Prospective Payment Systems and /Rates and Costs of Graduate Medical Education, Fiscal Year 2001 Rates; Final Rule.*" Wednesday, August 1, 2001

Federal Register, Department of Health and Human Services-Center for Medicare and Medicaid Services. Medicare Program, "*Prospective Payment System for Long-Term Hospitals; Implementation and FY 2003 Rates: Final Rule.*" Friday, August 30, 2002.

Hospital Chargemaster Guide
Ingenix Publishing Group. Reston, VA. 2001.

Johns, Merida L,
Health Information Management Technology: An Applied Approach
American Health Information Management Association. Chicago, IL, 2002.

Jones, Lolita,
Reimbursement Methodologies for Healthcare Services
American Health Information Management Association. Chicago, IL. 2001.

LaTour, Kathleen, Eichenwald, Shirley,
Health Information Management: Concepts, Principles, and Practice
American Health Information Management Association. Chicago, IL 2002.

Rowell, JoAnn C. and Green, Michelle A.
Understanding Health Insurance: A Guide to Professional Billing, 6th edition
Delmar Publishers, 2002.

Schraffenberger, LouAnn, et al,
Effective Management of Coding Service
American Health Information Management Association. Chicago, IL. 2002.

Medicare Payment Systems and Coding Files, http://cms.hhs.gov/paymentsystems/
This website provides links to pages containing official informational materials on the following Medicare payment systems and coding files:

Payment Systems

Ambulance Fee Schedule
Ambulatory Surgical Centers (ASC)
Ambulatory Surgical Center (ASC) Base Eligibility File
Berenson-Eggers Type of Service (BETOS) File
Clinical Lab Fee Schedule
Laboratory Public Meeting: Payment for 2004 New Clinical Laboratory Tests
Durable Medical Equipment, Prosthetics/Orthotics, and Supplies (DMEPOS) Fee Schedule
End Stage Renal Disease (ESRD) Program
Files for Download (formerly known as Public Use Files)
Home Health Prospective Payment System
Hospice Payment System
Hospital Inpatient Prospective Payment System
Hospital Outpatient Prospective Payment System
Inpatient Rehabilitation Facility Prospective Payment System
Long-Term Care Hospitals Prospective Payment System
Medicare PPS Excluded Cancer Hospitals
National Physician Fee Schedule Relative Value File
Physician Fee Schedule
Physician Fee Schedule Payment Amount File National/Carrier
Prospective Payment System (PPS) PC PRICER
Skilled Nursing Facility (SNF) Prospective Payment System

Coding Files

Alpha-Numeric HCPCS File
FY 2003 Updates to the ICD-9-CM Diagnosis Codes Effective October 1, 2002
Healthcare Common Procedure Coding System (HCPCS)
ICD-9-CM Coordination and Maintenance Committee
Place of Service Codes for Professional Claims
Zip code to Carrier Locality File

ICD-9-CM CODING

I. General Information
A. ICD-9-CM is a statistical classification and contains a category for <u>all</u> diagnoses and procedures.
B. The index contains unacceptable terminology as well as acceptable terminology. The index may contain several entries for a disease.
C. The Tabular List contains only one entry for each disease. A disease can be classified only once.
D. The digits in a code number are referred to as "rubrics".

II. Overview of Volumes and Conventions
A. Volume I - Tabular List
1. Diseases are listed only once in this volume (uses Rubrics 3, 4 or 5)
2. Divisions are
a. Chapter
b. Section
c. Category
d. Subcategory
e. 5th digits
3. Conventions:
a. Instructional Terms
i. Code also
ii. Excludes
iii. Includes
iv. Note
v. Use additional code
b. Punctuation Marks
i. Brace
ii. Brackets or Boxes
iii. Colon
iv. Parentheses
c. Abbreviations
i. NOS
ii. NEC
d. Symbols
i. Lozenge
ii. Section Mark
4. Appendices
a. Appendix A   Morphology of Neoplasms
b. Appendix B   Glossary of Mental Disorders
c. Appendix C   Classification of Drugs by the American Hospital Formulary Service List
d. Appendix D   Classification of Industrial Accidents According to Agency
e. Appendix E   List of Three-Digit Categories

B. Volume II - Alphabetic Index
1. Main Terms (conditions)
2. Subterms
3. Carryover Lines
4. Code Numbers and Morphology numbers
5. With
6. Due to
7. Conventions
   a. Instructional Terms
      i. Note
      ii. See
      iii. See also
      iv. See category
   b. Punctuation Marks
      i. Parentheses
      ii. Slanted Brackets
   c. Abbreviations
      i. NEC
8. Tables
   a. Neoplasm Table - Neoplasms arranged according to site and behavior.
   b. Table of Drugs and Chemicals - Hospital Formulary List
   c. Hypertension Table - Assumes relationship between hypertension and heart and/or kidney disease
9. Other Indices
   a. E code Index
C. Volume III - Procedure Tabular List and Alphabetic Index
1. Alphabetic Index:
   a. Format
      i. by
      ii. for
2. Tabular List: Rubrics - three or four
   a. Omit code
   b. Code also

III. Procedures for Coding Diseases and Procedures

  A. Diagnostic Coding
    1. Identify all main terms in the diagnostic statement.
    2. Locate each main term in the alphabetic index.
    3. Refer to subterms.
    4. Follow any cross-reference instructions given.
    5. Remember to be guided by instructional terms.
    6. Verify the code selected in the tabular list.
    7. Remember to be guided by instructional terms in the Tabular List.
    8. Assign codes to the highest level of specificity.
    9. Continue coding the diagnostic statement until all conditions are coded.

  B. Procedure Coding
    1. Identify all main terms in the procedural statement.
    2. Locate each main term in the alphabetic index.
    3. Refer to any subterms indented under the main term.
    4. Follow cross-reference instructions.
    5. Verify the code selected in the Tabular List.
    6. Read and be guided by instructional terms in the Tabular List.
    7. Continue coding the procedural statement until all component elements are fully identified.
    8. In the event a surgical procedure is begun and not completed due to unforeseen circumstances, code the procedure as far as the procedure progressed.
    9. Always code a biopsy even when the biopsied organ is removed.
    10. If there is no code for a bilateral procedure, list the procedure twice.

IV. Chapters
   A. Chapter 1 - Infectious and Parasitic Diseases
      1. Predominantly Communicable Diseases
      2. Combination and Multiple Codes
         a. code condition
         b. code organism
      3. Septicemia – Septic Shock
      4. Tuberculosis
      5. HIV – AIDS
      6. Late Effects of Infectious and Parasitic Diseases
   B. Chapter 2 – Neoplasms
      1. Neoplasm Table in Alphabetic Index
         a. Neoplasm Behavior
            i.   Malignant
            ii. Primary
            iii. Secondary
            iv. In situ
            v.   Benign
            vi. Uncertain behavior
            vii. Unspecified nature
      2. Morphology Codes located in Alphabetic Index
         a. Five digits
         b. First four digits indicate histology of neoplasm
         c. Fifth digit indicates behavior
      3. V Codes
         a. Radiation therapy and chemotherapy
         b. Personal history of malignancy
         c. Family history of malignancy
      4. Metastases
         a. Two sites must be coded—primary and metastatic site
         b. From
         c. To
         d. Spread to
         e. Extension from - to
         f. "From" or "of" usually considered primary site
         g. "Metastatic to" sites indicate secondary sites
   C. Chapter 3 - Endocrine and Metabolic Diseases and Immunity Disorders
      1. Diabetes Mellitus
         a. Fifth digit designations for IDDM, NIDDM and Uncontrolled
         b. Complications and Manifestations
            i. Alphabetic Index signifies principal diagnosis with slanted brackets enclosing secondary code.
      2. Hyperthyroidism
      3. Hypothyroidism
      4. Cystic Fibrosis

D. Chapter 4 - Diseases of the Blood and Blood Forming Organs
   1. Anemia
      a. Deficiency Anemias
         i.   Iron-deficiency (most common type)
         ii. Acute post hemorrhagic anemia
         iii. Pernicious anemia
         iv. Folate deficiency
      b. Hemolytic Anemias
      c. Thalassemia
      d. Sickle cell trait and sickle cell disease
   2. Coagulation Defects
E. Chapter 5 – Mental Disorders
   1. Psychoses
   2. Neuroses
   3. Personality Disorders
   4. Mental Retardation
   5. Alcoholism and alcohol abuse
   6. Drug dependence and abuse
F. Chapter 6 - Diseases of the Nervous System and Sense Organs
   1. Coding of epilepsy requires a fifth digit designating whether or not it is intractable.
   2. CVA
G. Chapter 7 - Diseases of the Circulatory System
   1. Use of the hypertension table
   2. Hypertensive "due to" indicates a causative factor.
   3. "And" or "With" hypertension indicate no link or causative factor for heart disease.
   4. Hypertension mentioned with renal disease can be assumed to be related.
   5. Myocardial infarction
      a. episode of care indicated by fifth digit
   6. Coronary Artery Disease
   7. Heart Failure
   8. Cerebral Vascular Disease
   9. Cardiovascular Procedures
      a. Cardiac Catheterization
      b. PTCA
      c. CABG
      d. Cardiac Pacemakers
H. Chapter 8 - Diseases of the Respiratory System
   1. Asthma
   2. Respiratory Failure
   3. COPD
   4. Pneumonia
   5. Bronchitis
   6. Bronchiectasis

I.   Chapter 9 – Diseases of the Digestive System
J.   Chapter 10 – Diseases of the Genitourinary System
K.   Chapter 11 – Complications of Pregnancy, Childbirth and the Puerperium
   1.   Definitions
      a.   Perinatal period
      b.   Postpartum period
      c.   Postnatal period
      d.   Antepartum period
      e.   Puerperium
      f.   Prematurity
      g.   Postpartum hemorrhage
      h.   Light for dates
   2.   Abortions
      a.   Fourth Digit Subclassification
         i.   Legal
         ii. Illegal
         iii. Spontaneous
      b.   Fifth Digit Subclassification
         i.   Complete
         ii. Incomplete
   3.   Requirements for normal pregnancy and delivery code (650)
      a.   Full term infant by weight and dates (2500 grams) (38 weeks- 10 lunar months)
      b.   Delivered with only a manual assist (no forceps or surgery)
      c.   Episiotomy allowed
      d.   Length of labor and delivery normal
      e.   Loss of blood less than 500 m.
      f.   Occiput (vertex) presentation of infant
      g.   No complications preceding and/or following labor
   4.   Fifth digits are required for most pregnancy codes
      a.   fifth digit 1 means delivered with or without an antepartum condition (most common fifth digit)
      b.   fifth digit 2 means delivered with postpartum condition
      c.   fifth digit 3 is used for undelivered pregnancy with antepartum condition
      d.   fifth digit 4 is used for undelivered pregnancy with postpartum condition
   5.   Pregnancy – Delivery Main Terms
      a.   Labor
      b.   Pregnancy
      c.   Delivery
      d.   Specific Complication
   6.   Outcome of delivery codes may be assigned but are never the principal diagnosis (V27).
L.   Chapter 12 – Diseases of the Skin and Subcutaneous Tissue
M.   Chapter 13 - Diseases of the Musculoskeletal System and Tissues
   1.   Pathological Fracture
   2.   Osteoporosis

N. Chapter 14 – Congenital Anomalies
O. Chapter 15 – Newborn (Perinatal) Guidelines
   1. General Perinatal Rule
   2. Use of Codes V30-V39
   3. Use of Category V29
   4. Maternal Causes of Perinatal Morbidity
   5. Congenital Anomalies
   6. Coding of Additional Perinatal Diagnoses
   7. Prematurity and Fetal Growth Retardation
P. Chapter 16 – Signs Symptoms and Ill Defined Conditions
Q. Chapter 17 - Injury and Poisoning
   1. Burns
      a. Definitions
         i. First Degree
         ii. Second Degree
         iii. Third Degree
      b. When assigning codes to burns, code burns to each site individually but only to the greatest degree
      c. Assign extent of burn codes when known.
         i. The fourth digit represents percent of body affected by burn.
         ii. The fifth digit represents percent of body with third degree burns.
   2. Multiple Injuries
      a. the most serious injury is designated as principal.
   3. Fractures and Dislocations
      a. Open
      b. Closed
   4. Poisoning and Adverse Effects of Chemicals
      a. Definition of poisoning
      b. Definition of adverse effect
      c. When coding an adverse effect, code the manifestation followed by the E code from the Therapeutic column on the Table of Drugs and Chemicals.
      d. When coding a poisoning, locate the drug or chemical in the Table and code the ICD-9-CM code first, followed by the E code from the Poisoning Sections of the Table.
   5. Complications of Medical and Surgical Care
   6. Late Effects
      a. Disabilities that require treatment after initial disease has subsided
      b. The defect is listed in the principal diagnosis position followed by late effect
R. V Codes – Factors Influencing Health Status and Contact with Health Services
   1. Key Main Terms
      a. Admission
      b. Examination
      c. History
      d. Observation
      e. Aftercare
      f. Problem
      g. Status

2. V codes used as principal diagnosis codes
    a. Aftercare of a resolving disease or injury
    b. Admission solely for chemotherapy and/or radiation therapy
    c. Dialysis
    d. Encounters for specific reason of person not currently ill
        i. organ donor
        ii. prophylactic care
        iii. counseling
    e. Indicating birth status of newborns (V30)
3. V codes as additional diagnosis codes
    a. to indicate that a person not currently ill has a history, health status or other problem that is not an illness or injury but may affect patient care
    b. to indicate the outcome of delivery for obstetric patients
S. E Codes – External Causes of Injury and Poisoning
    1. E codes capture
        a. how the injury or poisoning happened (cause)
        b. the intent
        c. place where event occurred
    2. Alphabetic Index
        a. follows Table of Drugs and Chemicals in ICD-9-CM codebook
        b. organization by main terms describing accident, circumstance, event or specific agent that caused the injury
    3. General E Code Guidelines
        a. Assign the appropriate E code for all initial treatments of an injury, poisoning or adverse effect of drugs.
        b. Use the late effect E code for subsequent visits when a late effect of the initial injury or poisoning is being treated. There is no late effect E code for adverse effects of drugs.
        c. Use the full range of E codes to completely describe the cause, intent and place of occurrence (if applicable) for all injuries, poisonings and adverse effects of drugs.
        d. Assign as many E codes as necessary to fully explain each external cause. If only one E code can be recorded, assign the one most related to the principal diagnosis.
        e. Select appropriate E codes by referring to the Index to External Causes and by reading inclusion and exclusion notes in the Tabular List.
    4. Multiple-Cause Coding Guidelines for E Codes
        a. E codes for child and adult abuse take priority over all other E codes, except as described in the child and adult abuse guidelines.
        b. E codes for cataclysmic events take priority over all other E codes, except for child and adult abuse.
        c. E codes for transport accidents take priority over all other E codes, except for cataclysmic events and for child and adult abuse.

ICD-9-CM Coding References

Health Information: Management of a Strategic Resource, 2nd edition
    Author: M. Abdelhak, et al. Publisher: W. B. Saunders

ICD-9-CM Coding Handbook with Answers, 2004 Revised Edition
    Author: Faye Brown Publisher: American Hospital Association

Step by - Step - Medical Coding, 4th edition
    Author: Carol Buck Publisher: W. B. Saunders

Basic ICD-9-CM Coding, 2004 Edition
    Author: Lou Anne Schraffenberger, MBA, RHIA, CCS, CCS-P Publisher: AHIMA

Coding Clinic for ICD-9-CM
    Publisher: American Hospital Association

ICD-9-CM Code Book with October 2003 updates
    Channel Publishing, Ltd.
    INGENIX

Understanding Medical Coding: A Comprehensive Guide
    Author: Sandra, L. Johnson Publisher: Delmar

Understanding Health Insurance: A Guide to Professional Billing, 6th Edition, 2002
    Author: JoAnn C. Rowell and Michelle A. Green Publisher: Delmar

CPT CODING

I. Format of CPT 2004
  A. Major Sections
    1. Evaluation/Management Services
    2. Anesthesia
    3. Surgery
    4. Radiology
    5. Pathology and Laboratory
    6. Medicine
  B. Subdivision of Major Sections
    1. Subsection/Category
    2. Subcategory
    3. Heading
    4. Procedure
    5. Categories, Subcategories and Headings identify
      a. services
      b. procedures or therapies
      c. examinations or tests
      d. body systems
  C. Conventions
    1. Semicolon (;)
      a. Common portion of main entry proceeds
      b. Indented information refers to common portion
    2. Bullet (•)
      a. New code number
    3. Triangle (▲)
      a. Revision to narrative description of a code number
    4. Facing Triangles (►◄)
      a. Indicates the beginning and ending of new and/or revised text with the guidelines and instructions
    5. Plus Sign (+)
      a. add on code
      b. not to be used alone
      c. primary procedure and add-on need to be performed by same physician
    6. Symbol (∅)
      a. indicates code that cannot be appended by modifier -51
  D. Code Categories in CPT
    1. Category I Codes
      a. traditional five digit CPT codes
    2. Category II Codes
      a. alphanumeric – 4 numbers followed by F
      b. tracking codes used for performance measurements
      c. use is optional
      d. located behind the Medicine Section

3. Category III Codes
    a. alphanumeric – 4 numbers followed by T
    b. temporary codes identify emerging technology services
    c. follow Category II codes
E. Characteristics of CPT
    1. Unlisted Procedure Code is used when no code can be found for a procedure
    2. Guidelines
        a. Specific Guidelines are located at the beginning of each chapter.
    3. Modifiers
        a. Added to CPT code numbers to signify
            i. Service/procedure has both professional and technical component
            ii. Service/procedure was performed by more than one physician and/or in more than one location
            iii. Service/procedure has been increased or reduced in scope
            iv. Service was performed partially
            v. Adjunct service was performed
            vi. Bilateral procedure was performed
            vii. Service/procedure was performed more than once
            viii. Unusual event occurred during the service/procedure
        b. Complete List of Modifiers Found in Appendix A of CPT 2004 Code Book
        c. Physician Use of CPT Modifiers
            i. Reported as two digits attached to code with a dash
            ii. Method preferred by AMA and CMS
            iii. Some third-party payers request that –50 modifier for bilateral procedure be used. Reported by repeating the procedure code twice and adding –50 to second code.
        d. Physician Use of HCPCS Level II Modifiers
            i. Two digit alphanumeric identifies
                o Specific finger or toe involved
                o Visit for second or third opinion
                o Service by someone other than physician
        e. Right or left side involvement
        f. Hospital Use of Modifiers
            i. CPT modifiers available for use by hospitals for outpatient Medicare services
                o two digit modifiers attached to CPT code with a dash
                o HCPCS Level II codes attached to CPT code with a dash
        g. CPT Modifiers Used With Surgical Codes.
    4. Notes
        a. Located at various levels such as the beginning of each section
        b. May identify integral components of a service or procedure
        c. May define terms and/or codes
        d. May direct the assignment of additional codes

II. Alphabetic Index
  A. Located at rear of CPT Manual
  B. Organization
     1. Main terms appear in bold print
     2. Main terms can include
        a. Procedure, service or examination
        b. Organ or anatomic site
        c. Condition or diagnosis
        d. Synonym
        e. Eponym
        f. Abbreviation
     3. Subterms
        a. Provide additional information required before selecting a code
     4. Cross-references
        a. "See" –refers a coder to another main term
        b. "See also"—refers a coder to another main term only if all the information sought did not follow the first main term
     5. Single code following main term
     6. Codes followed by commas
     7. Codes indicating a range use a dash (-) to separate first and last codes in the range

III. CPT Coding Rules
  A. Analyze the note or procedural statement.
  B. Determine the procedure, test or service to be coded.
  C. Locate the main term in the index.
  D. Review and select subterms.
  E. Note the code number(s) found opposite the selected main term or subterm.
     1. If a single code number is provided, locate that number in the body of the CPT Manual and verify.
     2. If two or more codes separated by a comma are shown, locate each code in the body of the CPT Manual and select the appropriate code.
     3. If a range of codes is shown, locate that range in the body of CPT and review all before selecting one.
  F. Note and follow all cross-references.
  G. Read all notes that apply to the code selected.
  H. Select appropriate modifier.
  I. Continue coding all components of the service/procedure.
  J. Never code directly from the Index.

IV. Evaluation and Management Services
A. Divided into Categories and Subcategories
B. Broad Categories
1. Office or Other Outpatient Services
2. Hospital Observation Services
3. Observation or Inpatient Care Services
4. Hospital Inpatient Services
5. Consultations
6. Emergency Department Services
7. Pediatric Critical Care Patient Transport
8. Critical Care Services
9. Nursing Facility Services
10. Domiciliary, Rest Home or Custodial Care Services
11. Home Services
12. Prolonged Services
13. Case Management Services
14. Care plan Oversight Services
15. Preventive Medicine Services
16. Newborn Care
17. Special Evaluation and Management Services
18. Other E/M Services
C. Basic Format of Code Numbers
1. Unique code numbers beginning with 99
2. Identify type or place of care
3. Define extent or level of service
4. Describe nature of presenting problem
5. Identify time typically required to provide service
D. Basic Information Required for Code Assignment
1. Type of Service
2. Place of Service
3. New or Established Patient
   a. New patient
      i. one who has not received professional services from physician or practice during the past three years
   b. Established Patient
      i. one who has received services during the past three years

E. Levels of Service (3-5 levels of service codes)
  1. Key Components must be documented
    a. History
       i. Problem focused
       ii. Expanded problem focused
       iii. Detailed
       iv. Comprehensive
    b. Examination
       i. Problem focused
       ii. Expended problem focused
       iii. Detailed
       iv. Comprehensive
    c. Medical Decision Making
       i. Straightforward
       ii. Low complexity
       iii. Moderate complexity
       iv. High complexity
       v. Contributing Components
          ○ Counseling and coordination of care
          ○ Nature of presenting problem
          ○ Time

V. Surgical Section
  A. Surgical Package (Global Surgical Concept) Inpatient
    1. Services Included:
      a. one evaluation and management (E/M) encounter the day prior to or the day of surgery
      b. surgical procedure
      c. local or topical anesthesia
      d. immediate postoperative care
      e. writing orders
      f. post anesthesia evaluation
      g. typical post-operative follow-up care
         i. Medicare guidelines differ
         ii. does not apply in the hospital outpatient setting
  B. Medicare definition for global surgical package for "major" procedures
    1. Preoperative services (one day prior to surgery)
    2. Actual procedure
    3. Postoperative services within 90 days following procedure
    4. Insignificant services not performed in OR
  C. Medicare Global Surgery Definition for Minor Procedures
    1. Preoperative Services
    2. Actual procedure
    3. Postoperative care (0-10 days)
  D. Separate Procedure
  E. Modifiers
    1. Appear in Guidelines of Surgical Section

F. Integumentary Subsection
  1. Excision of Benign versus Malignant Lesions
  2. Wound Repair/Closure
      a. Types of wound repair
          i.   Simple
          ii. Intermediate
          iii. Complex
      b. Rule for multiple wounds
  3. Skin Grafting
      a. Advancement
      b. Pedicle graft
      c. Z-plasty
      d. W-plasty
      e. V-Y plasty
      f. Rotational flap
G. Surgical Procedures of the Breast
  1. Breast Biopsy
      a. Incisional
      b. Excisional
      c. Needle
  2. Mastectomy
      a. Partial
      b. Simple, complete
      c. Subcutaneous
      d. Radical
      e. Modified radical
H. Musculoskeletal Subsection
  1. Fractures and Dislocations
      a. Open treatment
      b. Closed treatment
      c. Percutaneous skeletal fixation
      d. Manipulation
  2. Application of Casts and Strapping
  3. Arthroscopy
I. Respiratory Subsection
  1. Nasal Sinus Endoscopy
  2. Laryngoscopy
  3. Bronchoscopy
J. Cardiovascular Subsection
  1. Arterial Catheterizations
      a. Selective
      b. Nonselective
  2. Venous Catheterizations
      a. Selective
      b. Nonselective
  3. CABG
      a. arterial grafts
      b. venous grafts
  3. Pacemakers and Defibrillators
  4. Central Venous Access Procedures
      a. Centrally inserted catheter
      b. Peripherally inserted catheter

CPT Only © 2003 American Medical Association

K. Digestive Subsection
   1. Endoscopies
   2. Herniorrhaphy
     a. type
     b. age of patient
     c. history of recurrent hernia
     d. clinical presentation
       i. reducible
       ii. sliding
       iii. strangulated
       iv. incarcerated
L. Urinary Subsection
   1. Endoscopies
   2. Urodynamics
M. Male Genital Subsection
N. Laparoscopy / Peritoneoscopy / Hysteroscopy Subsection
O. Female Genital System Subsection
   1. Surgery involving female reproductive organs
   2. Maternity Care
   3. Delivery Services
P. Nervous System Subsection
   1. Contains codes for Craniotomy and Craniectomy
   2. Nerve block codes for pain management
   3. Laminotomy and Laminectomy
   4. Injection
Q. Eye and Ocular Adnexa Subsection
   1. Many refractive procedures are categorized in the unlisted section
   2. Cataract Extraction
     a. intracapsular
     b. extracapsular
     c. combination codes for cataract removal and insertion of lens
R. Auditory System Subsection
   1. Diagnostic Services such as audiometry found in Medicine Section

VI. Radiology
A. Use of Chargemaster for Billing
B. Radiological Supervision and Interpretation
C. Diagnostic Radiology
   1. X-ray
   2. CT Scan
   3. MRI
   4. MRA
D. Interventional Radiology
E. Diagnostic Ultrasound
   1. A-mode
   2. M-mode
   3. B-scan
   4. Real-time Scan

F. Radiation Oncology
    1. Consultation
    2. Clinical Treatment Planning
    3. Radiation Treatment Delivery
        a. Information needed for coding
            i.   number of treatment areas involved
            ii. number of ports involved
            iii. number of shielding blocks used
            iv. total million electron volts (MeV) administered
    4. Hyperthermia
    5. Clinical Brachytherapy
G. Nuclear Medicine
    1. Bone scans
    2. Cardiac scans
    3. Hepatobiliary scans
    4. Lung scans
    5. Renal scans
    6. Thyroid scans

VII. Pathology and Laboratory
A. Laboratory
    1. Alphabetic Index Listings
        a. Specific name of test
        b. Specific substance
        c. Specific method used
    2. Quantitative and Qualitative Studies
    3. Organ or Disease-Oriented Panels
    4. Evocative / Suppression Testing
    5. Chemistry
    6. Hematology and Coagulations
B. Surgical Pathology
    1. Gross Exam
    2. Microscopic Exam
    3. Index tissue to be examined

CPT Only © 2003 American Medical Association

VIII. Medicine

A. Specialty Services and Procedures
1. Immunizations
2. Therapeutic or Diagnostic Infusions
3. Therapeutic, Prophylactic or Diagnostic Injections
4. Psychiatry
    a. General Clinical diagnosis or Evaluation
    b. Psychiatric Therapy
5. Dialysis
6. Ophthalmology
    a. Services
        i. New Patient
        ii. Established Patient
        iii. Intermediate
        iv. Comprehensive
        v. Contact Lens
        vi. Spectacles
B. Special Otorhinolaryngology Services
C. Cardiovascular
1. Services
    a. Stent placement
    b. Coronary Angioplasty
    c. Coronary Atherectomy
D. Pulmonary
E. Allergy and Clinical Immunology
1. Allergy Sensitivity Tests
2. Immunotherapy
F. Neurology and Neuromuscular Procedures and CNS Assessment Tests
G. Health and Behavior Assessments / Intervention
H. Chemotherapy Administration
I. Special Dermatological Procedures
J. Physical Medicine and Rehabilitation
K. Osteopathic Manipulative Treatment
L. Chiropractic Manipulative Treatment
M. Qualifying Circumstances for Anesthesia
N. Sedation with or without Analgesia
O. Other Services and Procedures
P. Home Health Procedures / Services
Q. Home Infusion Procedures

IX. Anesthesia
   A. Anesthesia Services
      1. General
      2. Regional
      3. Local
   B. Range of Service
      1. Usual pre- and postoperative visits
      2. Anesthesia
      3. Administration of fluids or blood
      4. Usual monitoring services
   C. Developed for billing for anesthesiologists
   D. Anesthesia Modifiers
      1. Modifiers describe patient physical status
   E. Some third-party-payers require use of surgical code plus anesthesia modifier
   F. Locate anesthesia codes in the Index by referencing "anesthesia"
   G. Anesthesia codes are used for anesthesiologist's professional billing (not used for hospital billing)

X. Miscellaneous
   A. National Correct Coding Initiative (NCCI) or Correct Coding Initiative (CCI)
      1. Comprehensive Component Edit
         a. HCPCS that should not be used together
         b. Listed in table
      2. Mutually Exclusive Edit
         a. Impossible or improbable combinations of codes
         b. Included in most encoding software
   B. HCPCS Level II Codes (National Codes)
      1. Five Digit Alphanumeric Codes (A through V excluding S)
      2. Developed by CMS to report physician and non-physician services not covered sufficiently in CPT
      3. Includes such services as:
         a. Drugs (J Codes)
         b. Durable Medical Equipment
         c. Ambulance Services
         d. Orthotic / Prosthetic Procedures
      4. Includes Modifiers that May be used with Level II or CPT Codes
      5. General Guidelines
         a. never code from the index
         b. search for Main Terms and any applicable Subterms
         c. note the Reference codes in the Index
         d. verify codes by reading entire description

CPT Coding References

Health Information: Management of a Strategic Resource, 2nd edition
   Author: M. Abdelhak, et al   Publisher: W. B. Saunders

Step by - Step - Medical Coding, 4th edition
   Author: Carol Buck   Publisher: W. B. Saunders

Physician's Current Procedural Terminology CPT 2004
   Publisher: American Medical Association

HCPCS Medicare's National Level II Codes (2004)
   Publisher: American Medical Association

CPT Assistant
   Publisher: American Medical Association

Understanding Medical Coding A Comprehensive Guide
   Author: Sandra, L. Johnson   Publisher: Delmar

Understanding Health Insurance: A Guide to Professional Billing, 6th Edition. (2002)
   Author: JoAnn C. Rowell and Michelle A. Green   Publisher: Delmar

Medical Science

I. General Concepts of Disease
A. Major Categories of Disease
1. Congenital and Hereditary
2. Inflammatory
3. Degenerative
4. Metabolic
5. Neoplastic
B. Principles of Diagnosis
1. History
2. Physical Examination
3. Diagnostic Tests and Procedures
   a. Clinical Laboratory Tests
   b. Tests of Electrical Activity
   c. Radioisotope Studies
   d. Endoscopy
   e. Ultrasound
   f. X-ray Examination
   g. Magnetic Resonance Imaging
   h. Positron Emission Tomography
   i. Cytologic and Histologic Examinations

II. Pathology of Disease
A. Structure and Function of Cells and Tissues
B. Chromosomes, Genes and Cell Division
C. Inflammation and Repair
1. Acute Inflammation
   a. Clinical Manifestation
      i. Hyperemia and Heat
      ii. Swelling
      iii. Pain
2. Outcomes of Inflammatory Reactions
   a. Resolution and Healing
      i. Resolution with Abnormal Healing
         • Keloid
         • Adhesions
3. Tissue Damage
   a. Rheumatic Fever
   b. Systemic Lupus Erythematosus
4. Chemical Mediators of Inflammation
5. Suppression of Inflammation
   a. Indications
   b. Therapy

III. Pathologenic Microorganisms – Animal Parasites – Communicable Diseases
  A. Pathogenic Microorganisms
    1. Bacteria
      a. Classification
        i. identification
          * shape
          * grain stain
          * biochemical and cultural
          * structural
    2. Viruses
      a. Classification
      b. Mode of action
      c. Bodily Defenses
    3. Chlamydiae
    4. Rickettsiae
    5. Mycoplasmas
    6. Fungi
  B. Animal Parasites
    1. Protozoal Infestations
    2. Metazoal Infestations
    3. Arthropods
  C. Communicable Diseases
    1. Methods of Transmission
      a. Direct
      b. Indirect
    2. Methods of Control
      a. Immunization
      b. Identification, Isolation and Treatment of Infected Persons
      c. Control of Means of Indirect Transmission
    3. Sexually Transmitted Diseases
      a. Syphilis
        i. Stages
          * primary
          * secondary
          * tertiary
        ii. Congenital
      b. Gonorrhea
      c. Herpes
    4. Human Immunodeficiency Virus Infections and AIDS

IV. Congenital and Hereditary Diseases
- A. Chromosomal Abnormalities
  1. Sex chromosome abnormalities
     - a. Turner's syndrome
     - b. Triple X syndrome
     - c. Klinefelter's syndrome
     - d. XYY syndrome
  2. Abnormalities of Autosomes
     - a. Down's syndrome
- B. Genetically Determined Diseases
  1. Transmission
     - a. autosomal (dominant, recessive or co-dominant)
     - b. sex-linked
  2. Phenylketonuria
  3. Tay-Sachs
  4. Cystic fibrosis
  5. Sickle cell anemia
  6. Hemophilia
- C. Intrauterine Injury
- D. Interaction of Genetic and Environment Factors
- E. Prenatal Diagnosis
  1. Application
  2. Technique

V. Neoplastic Disease
- A. Classification and Nomenclature
  1. Benign tumors
  2. Malignant tumors
     - a. Carcinoma
     - b. Sarcoma
     - c. Leukemia
- B. Comparison of Benign and Malignant Tumors
  1. Growth Rate
  2. Character of Growth
  3. Tumor Spread
  4. Cell Differentiation
- C. Etiology of Neoplastic Disease
  1. Viruses
  2. Precancerous Conditions
  3. Gene Chromosomal Abnormalities
  4. Failure of Immunologic Defenses
  5. Heredity and Tumors
- D. Diagnosis of Tumors
  1. Early Recognition
  2. Cytologic Diagnosis
  3. Frozen-Section Diagnosis
  4. Tumor-Associated Antigen Tests

E. Treatment of Tumors
    1. Surgery
    2. Radiotherapy
    3. Hormones
    4. Anticancer Drugs
    5. Adjuvant Chemotherapy
    6. Immunotherapy
F. Leukemia
    1. Classification
    2. Clinical Features
    3. Principles of Treatment
    4. Preleukemia/Myelodysplasia
G. Multiple Myeloma
H. Survival Rates in Neoplastic Disease
I. Cancer Programs
    1. Sponsor
    2. Essential features
    3. Purpose
    4. Abstracting
       a. locating information for abstract in medical record
       b. staging

VI. Abnormalities of Blood Coagulation
A. Factors concerned with hemostasis
    1. Blood vessels and platelets
    2. Plasma coagulation factors
       a. Phase 1
       b. Phase 2
       c. Phase 3
          i.   coagulation inhibitors
          ii. calcium
B. Clinical disturbances of blood coagulation
    1. Abnormalities of small blood vessels
    2. Deficiency of plasma coagulation factors
       a. First Phase
          i.   usually congenital
          ii. hemophilia
       b. Second Phase
          i.   anticoagulant Drugs
          ii. inadequate synthesis of vitamin K
          iii. inadequate absorption of vitamin K
          iv. severe liver disease
    3. Circulation of thromboplastic materials

C. Laboratory Tests to Evaluate Hemostasis
1. Platelets
   a. Platelet Count
2. Overall Evaluation of Coagulation Mechanism
   a. Clotting time - Whole Blood
   b. Partial Thromboplastin Time
   c. Second and Third Stages
      i. Prothrombin Time
   d. Third Stage
      i. Thrombin Time
      ii. Fibrinogen and Fibrin Degradation Products

VII. Circulatory Disturbances
A. Thrombosis and Embolism
1. Pathogenesis
2. Venous Thrombosis
3. Pulmonary Embolism
   a. Diagnostic Tests
      i. Chest X-Ray
      ii. Lung Scan
      iii. Pulmonary Angiography
   b. Treatment
      i. Anticoagulants
      ii. Surgical Interruption of Vena Cava
4. Arterial Thrombosis
5. Intracranial Thrombosis
6. Thrombosis Due to Increased Blood Coagulability
7. Embolism due to Foreign Material
B. Edema
1. Capillary and Interstitial Tissue Fluid
2. Pathogenesis
   a. Increased Capillary Permeability
   b. Low Plasma Proteins
   c. Increased Hydrostatic Pressure
      i. Heart Failure
      ii. Localized Venous Obstruction
   d. Lymphatic Obstructions

VIII. Cardiovascular System
A. Anatomy and Physiology of Cardiovascular System
1. Cardiac Chambers
2. Cardiac Valve
3. Blood Supply to Heart
4. Conduction System
5. Blood Pressure
B. Heart Disease as a Disturbance of Cardiac Function
1. Congenital Heart Disease
2. Valvular Heart Disease
   a. Rheumatic Fever and Rheumatic Heart Disease
   b. Nonrheumatic Aortic Stenosis
   c. Mitral Valve Prolapse
3. Infective Endocarditis

C. Coronary Heart Disease
  1. Pathogenesis of Atherosclerosis
  2. Manifestations and Complications
     a. Angina pectoris
     b. Heart Attack
  3. Diagnosis—angiography
  4. Treatment
     a. Medical
        i. drugs
        ii. reduction of risk factors
     b. Surgical
        i. Myocardial Revascularization
        ii. Coronary Angioplasty
D. Myocardial Infarction
  1. Complications
     a. Arrhythmias
     b. Heart Failure
     c. Intracardiac Thrombi
     d. Pericarditis
     e. Cardiac Rupture
     f. Papillary Muscle Dysfunction
     g. Ventricular Aneurysm
  2. Survival
  3. Diagnosis
     a. History and physical
     b. Electrocardiogram
     c. Enzyme tests
  4. Treatment
E. Hypertension
  1. Vascular Effects
  2. Etiology
  3. Treatment (drugs)
F. Primary Myocardial Disease
  1. Myocarditis
  2. Cardiomyopathy
G. Heart Failure
  1. Definition
  2. Pathogenesis
  3. Treatment
  4. Acute Pulmonary Edema
H. Aneurysm
  1. Arteriosclerotic
  2. Dissecting
I. Diseases of Veins
  1. Venous Thrombosis and Thrombophlebitis
  2. Varicose Veins (lower extremities)
     a. Complications
     b. Treatment
J. Other Varicosities
  1. Hemorrhoids
  2. Esophageal varices
  3. Varicocele

IX. The Hematopoietic and Lymphatic Systems
A. Composition and Function of Human Blood
B. Normal Hematopoiesis
C. Anemia
1. Etiologic Classification
2. Morphological Classification
a. Size of cells (normo, micro, macro)
b. Hemoglobin content - hypochromic
3. Iron-Deficiency Anemia
4. Folic Acid deficiency
5. Vitamin B12 deficiency
6. Bone Marrow Damage or Infiltration
7. Acute Blood Loss
8. Hemolytic Anemia
a. Hereditary
b. Acquired
9. Diagnostic Evaluation
D. Polycythemia
1. Secondary Polycythemia
2. Primary Polycythemia
E. Thrombocytopenia
1. Secondary
2. Primary
F. Structure and Function of the Lymphatic System
1. Lymph Nodes
2. Spleen
3. Thymus Development of the Lymphatic System
G. Diseases of the Lymphatic System
1. Lymphadenitis
2. Infectious Mononucleosis
3. Neoplasms
H. Alteration of the Immune Reaction in Diseases of Lymphatic System
I. Enlarged Lymph Nodes as Diagnostic Problem
J. Role of Spleen in Protection Against Systemic Infection
1. Functions of Spleen
2. Splenectomy
a. Indications
b. Effects
c. Post-Splenectomy Treatment

X. The Respiratory System
A. Structure of Lungs
1. Bronchi
2. Bronchioles
3. Alveoli
4. Pleura
B. Function of Lungs
1. Ventilation
2. Gas exchange
3. Pleural Cavity
4. Pulmonary Function Tests
   a. Vital capacity
   b. PO2 and PCO2
C. Pneumothorax
1. Signs and Symptoms
2. Tension pneumothorax
3. Treatment
D. Atelectasis
E. Pneumonia
1. Classification
2. Clinical Features
3. Pneumocystis Pneumonia
F. Tuberculosis
1. Manifestations
2. Diagnostic methods
3. Treatment
G. Bronchitis and Bronchiectasis
H. Chronic Obstructive Lung Disease (COPD)
1. Definition
2. Structure and Function changes
3. Prevention
4. Treatment
I. Bronchial Asthma
1. Pathogens
2. Treatment
J. Respiratory Distress Syndrome
1. Neonatal
2. Adult
K. Pulmonary Fibrosis
L. Lung Carcinoma

XI. The Gastrointestinal Tract
- A. Diseases of the Face and Oral Cavity
  1. Cleft Lip and Palate anomalies
  2. Abnormalities of Tooth Development
  3. Dental Caries and Complications
  4. Periodontal Disease
  5. Inflammation of the Oral Cavity
     a. Stomatitis
  6. Tumors of the Oral Cavity
     a. Carcinoma
- B. Diseases of the Esophagus
  1. Cardiac Sphincter Dysfunction
     a. Cardiospasm
     b. Incompetent Sphincter
  2. Mucosal Tears
  3. Carcinoma of Esophagus
  4. Food Impaction
  5. Stricture
- C. Peptic Ulcer
- D. Carcinoma of Stomach
- E. Intestinal Diseases
  1. Inflammatory Disease of the Intestine
     a. Acute Enteritis
     b. Chronic Enteritis
        i. complications
  2. Appendicitis
  3. Meckel's Diverticulum
  4. Disturbances of Bowel function Due to Food Intolerance
     a. Lactose Intolerance
     b. Gluten Intolerance
  5. Irritable Bowel Syndrome (Crohn's Disease)
  6. Diverticulosis and Diverticulitis of Colon
  7. Intestinal Obstruction
     a. High Intestinal Obstruction
     b. Low Intestinal Obstruction
- F. Mesenteric Thrombosis
- G. Tumors of the Bowel
  1. Small Intestine
  2. Colon
- H. Imperforate Anus
- I. Hemorrhoids
  1. Classification
  2. Treatment
- J. Diagnostic Evaluation of Gastrointestinal Tract Disease
  1. Endoscopy
  2. Biopsy
  3. X-Ray

XII. The Liver and Biliary System

A. Structure and Function of the Liver
 1. Size and Location
 2. Double Blood Supply
 3. Metabolism
   a. Protein
   b. Carbohydrate
   c. Lipid
 4. Filtering of Blood
 5. Synthesis, Storage and Release of Water Soluble Vitamins
 6. Regulates Blood Volume
 7. Detoxification
 8. Formation and Excretion of Bile
B. Liver Injury
 1. Viral hepatitis
   a. Hepatitis A
   b. Hepatitis B
   c. Non-A, Non-B Hepatitis
   d. Hepatitis D Delta Hepatitis
 3. Fatty Liver
 4. Alcoholic Hepatitis
 5. Cirrhosis
 6. Reye's Syndrome
C. Diseases of Gallbladder
 1. Cholelithiasis
 2. Cholecystitis
 3. Tumors of liver and gallbladder
 4. Jaundice

XIII. The Urinary System

A. Structure and Function of Urinary Tract/Kidney
 1. Kidney
   a. Cortex
   b. Medulla
 2. Excretory Duct system
   a. Urethra
   b. Ureters
   c. Pelvis
 3. Bladder (storage)
 4. Functions of Kidney
B. Diseases of Urinary Tract
 1. Glomerulonephritis
 2. Nephrotic Syndrome
   a. Adults
   b. Children
 3. Arteriolar Nephrosclerosis
 4. Diabetic Nephropathy
 5. Urinary Tract Infection
   a. Cystitis
   b. Pyelonephritis
   c. Vesicoureteral Reflux
 6. Urinary Tract Calculi
 7. Foreign Bodies in the Urinary Tract

8. Renal Tubular Injury
9. Renal Cysts
   a. Solitary
   b. Multiple
   c. Wilms' Tumor
10. Renal Failure (uremia)
C. Diagnostic Evaluation of Kidney and Urinary Tract Disease
   1. Laboratory Tests
      a. Urinalysis
      b. Urine Culture and Sensitivity
      c. Blood Chemistry Tests
      d. Clearance Tests
   2. X-ray studies
      a. X-Ray of Abdomen
      b. Pyelogram
      c. CT Scan
      d. Arteriogram
   3. Ultrasound
   4. Cystoscopy
   5. Renal Biopsy
D. Treatment
   1. Extracorporeal Hemodialysis
   2. Peritoneal Dialysis
   3. Kidney Transplantation

XIV. The Pancreas and Diabetes Mellitus
A. Function of the Pancreas
   1. Exocrine function
   2. Endocrine function
      a. Islets of Langerhans cells secretions
B. Diseases of the Pancreas
   1. Acute Pancreatitis
   2. Chronic Pancreatitis
   3. Cystic Fibrosis of the Pancreas
   4. Diabetes Mellitus
      a. Type I IDDM
      b. Type II NIDDM
      c. Complications of Diabetes Mellitus
         i.   Increased Susceptibility to Infection
         ii.   Diabetic Coma
         iii. Ketoacidosis
         iv.   Hyperosmolar coma
         v.   Arteriosclerosis
         vi.   Blindness
         vii. Renal Failure
         viii. Peripheral Neuritis
   5. Hypoglycemia
   6. Tumors of the Pancreas

XV. Water, Electrolyte and Acid Base Balance
   A. Relationship of Intracellular and Extracellular Fluid
   B. Acid-Base Balance
   C. Physiologic Concepts
   D. Disturbances of Acid-Base Balance
      1. Metabolic Acidosis
      2. Respiratory Acidosis
      3. Metabolic Alkalosis
      4. Respiratory Alkalosis.
   E. Evaluation of Acid-Base Balance by the Clinician.
      1. Clinical Evaluation
      2. Laboratory Studies (pH, pCO_2, bicarbonate, blood gas studies)

XVI. Integumentary System
   A. Skin
      1. Epidermis
      2. Dermis
   B. Hair and Nails
   C. Disorders
      1. Burns
         a. Classification
            i. Body Surface Affected
            ii. Severity of Burns
      2. Wounds (Lacerations or Open Wounds)
         a. Closures
            i. Simple
            ii. Intermediate
            iii. Complex
            iv. Debridement
      3. Skin Infections
         a. Carbuncle and Furuncle
         b. Cellulitis and Abscess
      4. Other Inflammatory Conditions
         a. Contact Dermatitis
            i. Eczema
            ii. Rash
         b. Dermatitis due to Drugs
      5. Rashes due to Photosensitivity
      6. Lupus Erythematosus
      7. Pruritus
      8. Sebaceous Cyst
      9. Decubitus Ulcer
      10. Urticaria

XVII. The Nervous System
A. Structure and function of brain and nervous system
1. Meninges
2. Brain
3. Voluntary Muscles
B. Diseases of Nervous System
1. Muscle Paralysis
2. Closure Defects
a. Anencephaly
b. Spina Bifida
3. Prenatal Determination of Neural Tube Defect
C. Hydrocephalus
1. Congenital
D. Stroke
E. Infections
1. Systemic Infection
2. Bacterial Meningitis
3. Viral Infections
F. Alzheimer's Disease
G. Multiple Sclerosis
H. Parkinson's Disease
I. Tumors
1. Peripheral Nerve Tumors
2. Brain Tumors
3. Spinal Cord Tumors
J. Diseases of Peripheral Nerves
1. Injury
2. Polyneuritis
3. Guillain-Barré Syndrome
K. Neurological Manifestations of HIV
1. Viral meningitis
2. AIDS encephalopathy
3. Polyneuritis
4. Opportunistic Infections
a. Herpes
b. Cytomegalovirus
c. Toxoplasma Gondii
5. AIDS-related Tumors
a. Kaposi's Sarcoma
b. Lymphoma

XVIII. Musculo-Skeletal System
  A. Structure and Function of the skeletal system
    1. Bones
    2. Joints
    3. Cartilage
    4. Tendon
    5. Ligament
  B. Congenital Malformations of Skeletal System
    1. Achondroplasia
    2. Osteogenesis Imperfecta
    3. Polydactyly
    4. Talipes
    5. Congenital Dislocation of Hip
  C. Common Skeletal Diseases
    1. Arthritis
    2. Rheumatoid arthritis
    3. Osteoarthritis
    4. Gout
    5. Fractures
    6. Osteomyelitis
    7. Bone tumors
      a. Osteosarcoma
      b. Multiple myeloma
      c. Metastatic site
    8. Osteoporosis
    9. Intervertebral disk disease
  D. Structure and Function of Skeletal Muscles
    1. Structure
    2. Myoneural Junction
    3. Acetylcholine
  E. Muscular Diseases
    1. Myositis
    2. Muscular Dystrophy
    3. Myasthenia Gravis

XIX. Breast
  A. Structure and Physiology of breast
  B. Mammogram
  C. Abnormalities of Breast Development
    1. Accessory Breasts and Nipples
    2. Unequal Development
    3. Hypertrophy
    4. Gynecomastia
    5. Galactorrhea
  D. Other Diseases of the Breast
    1. Benign cystic Disease
    2. Fibroadenoma
    3. Carcinoma of Breast
    4. Sarcoma of Breast
  E. Lump in Breast
    1. Diagnostic possibilities
    2. Diagnostic approach

XX. The Female Reproductive System
A. Infections of the Genital Tract
1. Sexually transmitted diseases
2. Cervicitis
3. Salpingitis and PID
4. Condyloma
B. Endometriosis
C. Cervical carcinoma
D. Polyp
E. Uterine myomas
F. Dysmenorrhea
G. Cysts
H. Toxic Shock Syndrome
I. Contraception
1. Natural
2. Contraceptive pills
3. Diaphragm and Condoms
4. IUD

XXI. Diseases Associated with Pregnancy
A. Fertilization and Prenatal Development
1. Fertilization
2. Early Development
3. In Vitro Fertilization and Embryo Transfer
B. Duration of Pregnancy
1. Dated from Conception - 38 weeks
2. Dated from last menstrual period - forty weeks
C. Amniotic Fluid
1. Polyhydramnios
2. Oligohydramnios
D. Ectopic Pregnancy
1. Tubal Pregnancy
E. Hydatidiform Mole
F. Pregnancy with Abortive Outcome
1. Missed Abortion
2. Spontaneous
3. Induced (legal and illegal)
4. Complete
5. Incomplete
6. Complications of abortions
a. Genital Tract and Pelvic Infection
b. Delayed or Excessive Hemorrhage
c. Renal Failure
d. Metabolic Disorders
e. Shock
G. Complications Following Abortion, Ectopic and Molar Pregnancies
1. Complications of Pregnancy
a. Threatened Abortion
b. Missed Abortion
c. Placenta Previa
d. Premature Separation of Placenta

XXII. Pregnancy, Childbirth and Puerperium
   A. Abnormal Attachment of Umbilical Cord and Placenta
      1. Velamentous Insertion of Cord
      2. Placenta Previa
   B. Multiple Pregnancies
      1. Twin Transfusion Syndrome
      2. Blighted Twins
      3. Disadvantages of Twin Pregnancies
   C. Hemolytic Disease of the Newborn
      1. Rh Hemolytic Disease
      2. ABO Hemolytic Disease
   D. Stages of Pregnancy
      1. Prenatal
      2. Birth
      3. Postnatal
   E. Stages of Labor
   F. Diseases Complicating Pregnancy, Childbirth and Puerperium
      1. Benign Essential Hypertension
      2. Hypertension secondary to renal disease
      3. Syphilis
      4. Tuberculosis
      5. Malaria
      6. Rubella
      7. Diabetes mellitus
      8. Anemia
   G. Diseases of Pregnancy
      1. Excessive Vomiting in Pregnancy
      2. Early or Threatened Labor
      3. Early Onset of Delivery
      4. Prolonged Pregnancy
      5. Preeclampsia/Eclampsia
      6. Gestational diabetes
   H. Normal Delivery
   I. Malposition and Malpresentation of Fetus
      1. Breech Presentation
      2. Other Forms of Malpresentation
   J. Other Complications of Labor and Delivery
      1. Obstructed Labor
         a. Fetopelvic Disproportion
         b. Prior Cesarean Section
         c. Unusually Large Fetus Causing Disproportion
      2. Fetal Distress
      3. Advanced Maternal Age as Risk Factor
      4. Precipitate Labor
      5. Perineal Laceration
      6. Postpartum Hemorrhage
   K. Surgical Procedures Associated with Delivery
      1. Cesarean Section
      2. Manual Version of Fetus
      3. Episiotomy
      4. Suture of Lacerations of Perineum
      5. Forceps Delivery

References for Medical Sciences

The MERCK MANUAL of Diagnosis and Therapy
Published by: Merck and Co., Inc.
Rathway, NJ

American Medical Association Encyclopedia of Medicine
Published by: AMA
Chicago, IL

Taber's Cyclopedic Medical Dictionary
Published by: F. A. Davis Company
Philadelphia, PA

Boyd's Introduction to the Study of Disease
Published by: Lea and Febiger
Philadelphia, Pa

Pathology for the Health-Related Professions
Published by: W. B. Saunders Company
Philadelphia, PA

Mosby's Medica, Nursing, and Allied Health Dictionary
Published by: Mosby
St. Louis, MO

PHARMACOLOGY

I. Drug References
  A. Physician's Desk Reference (PDR)
  B. United States Pharmacopeia/Dispensing Information (USP/DI)
  C. American Health-System Formulary Service (AHFS)
  D. Compendium of Drug Therapy

II. Identification of Drugs in References
  A. Names
    1. Generic
    2. Official
    3. Trade
    4. Chemical
  B. Terms Applicable to Drugs
    1. Legal Terms
      a. Over-the-Counter (OTC)
      b. Legend
      c. Controlled Substance
    2. Terms Indicating Drug Actions
      a. Indications
      b. Actions
      c. Contraindications
      d. Warnings or Cautions
      e. Side Effects of Adverse Reactions
  C. Classifications
    1. Broad categories based on affect on body.
    2. Examples
      a. Antipyretic
      b. Antibiotic

III. Sources of Drugs
  A. Plants
  B. Minerals
  C. Animals
  D. Synthetic

IV. Drug Processing by the Body
A. Methods
  1. Absorption
  2. Distribution
  3. Metabolism
  4. Excretion
B. Variables
  1. Age
  2. Weight
  3. Sex
  4. Psychological State
  5. Drug Interactions
    a. Synergism
    b. Potentiation
    c. Antagonism
  6. Dosage
    a. Minimum Dose
    b. Maximum Dose
    c. Loading Dose
    d. Maintenance Dose
    e. Lethal Dose
    f. Therapeutic Dose
  7. Route
    a. GI Tract
      i. Oral (PO)
      ii. Nasogastric (NG)
      iii. Rectal (R)
    b. Parenteral
      i. Sublingual
      ii. Injection
        • Intravenous (IV)
        • Intramuscular (IM)
        • Subcutaneous (SC)
        • Intradermal (ID)
        • Intracardiac
        • Intraspinal
      iii. Topical
        • Dermal (D)
        • Mucosal
      iv. Inhalation
  8. Terms Referring to Adverse Effects
    a. Teratogenic Effect
    b. Idiosyncrasy
    c. Tolerance
    d. Dependence
    e. Hypersensitivity
    f. Anaphylactic Reaction

V. Medication Orders
A. Contents
1. Date
2. Patient's Name
3. Medication Name
4. Dosage or Amount of Medicine
5. Route or Manner of Administration
6. Time to Be Administered
B. Common Abbreviations
1. Time of Administration
2. Systems of Measurement
a. Apothecary System
b. Metric System

VI. Principles of Drug Administration (TRAMPD acronym)
A. Right Time
B. Right Route
C. Right Amount
D. Right Medication
E. Right Patient
F. Right Documentation

VII. Vitamins and Minerals
A. Fat-Soluble Vitamins
1. Vitamin A
2. Vitamin D
3. Vitamin E
4. Vitamin K
B. Water-Soluble Vitamins
1. Vitamin B_1
2. Vitamin B_2
3. Vitamin B_6
4. Vitamin B_{12}
5. Folic Acid
6. Vitamin C
C. Minerals
1. Sodium
2. Chloride
3. Potassium (K)
4. Calcium (CA)
5. Iron (FE)

VIII. Skin Medications
A. Classifications
1. Antipruritics
2. Emollients and Demulcents
3. Keratolytics
4. Scabicides and Pediculicides
5. Antifungals
6. Antivirals
7. Local Anti-Infectives
   a. Antiseptics
   b. Burn Medications

IX. Autonomic Nervous System Drugs
A. Classifications
1. Adrenergics
   a. Examples
      i. epinephrine (adrenalin)
      ii. dopamine
      iii. ephedrine
      iv. norepinephrine
2. Adrenergic Blockers
   a. Example - propranolol
3. Cholinergics
4. Cholinergic Blockers

X. Antineoplastic Drugs
A. Classifications
1. Antimetabolites
2. Plant Alkaloids
3. Antitumor Antibiotics
4. Alkylating Agents
5. Hormone Therapy
6. Interferons
7. Paclitaxel
8. Radioactive Isotopes

XI. Urinary System Drugs
A. Classifications
1. Diuretics (most common are Thiazides such as Diuril)
   a. Loop Diuretics
   b. Potassium-Sparing Diuretics (Aldactone)
   c. Osmotic Agents (Mannitol)
2. Medications for Gout
   a. Uricosuric Agents (probenecid)
   b. Allopurinol
3. Antispasmodics (neurogenic bladder, incontinence)
4. Analgesics - Phenazopyridine (urinary tract mucosa burning, itching, etc.)
5. Cholinergics - Bethanechol (contracts urinary bladder)
6. Treatment of Benign Prostatic Hypertrophy
   a. Proscar (to reduce prostate size)

XII. Gastrointestinal Drugs
  A. Classifications
    1. Antacids
    2. Antidiarrhea
    3. Antiflatulents
    4. Laxatives and Cathartics
    5. Stool Softeners
    6. Antiemetics

XIII. Anti-Infective Drugs
  A. Classifications
    1. Antibiotics
      a. Aminoglycosides (used for treatment of gram-negative infections)
      b. Cephalosporins (related to Penicillin)
      c. Chloramphenicol
      d. Erythromycins - least toxic of antibiotics (used in many respiratory infections)
      e. Penicillins
        i. used for treatment of streptococcal, staphylococcal and meningococcal infections
        ii. drug of choice for treatment of gonorrhea and syphilis
      f. Quinolones (ciprofloxacin)
      g. Tetracyclines (broad spectrum antibiotic)
        i. Antifungals
        ii. Antituberculosis Agents
        iii. Antivirals (acyclovir)
        iv. Antiretroviral (HIIV)
        v. Sulfonamides

XIV. Eye Medications
  A. Classifications
    1. Anti-Infectives
    2. Anti-Inflammatory Agents
    3. Antiglaucoma Agents
      a. Carbonic Anhydrase Inhibitors
      b. Miotics
      c. Beta-Adrenergic Blockers
      d. Sympathomimetics
    4. Mydriatics (atropine)
    5. Local Anesthetics

XV. Analgesics, Sedatives and Hypnotics
  A. Analgesics
    1. Opioid (Codeine)
    2. Nonopioid (aspirin, ASA, acetaminophen/Tylenol)
  B. Sedatives and Hypnotics
    1. Barbiturates
    2. Nonbarbiturates

XVI. Psychotropic Medications
  A. Classifications
    1. CNS Stimulants (caffeine, Ritalin)
    2. Antidepressants
       a. Tricyclics
       b. MAO Inhibitors
    3. Antimanic Agents
    4. Anxiolytics
    5. Antipsychotic Medications/Major Tranquilizers (Thorazine, Haldol)

XVII. Musculoskeletal and Anti-Inflammatory Drugs
  A. Skeletal Muscle Relaxants
  B. Anti-Inflammatory Drugs
    1. Nonsteroidal
  C. Osteoporosis Therapy (Fosamax)

XVIII. Anticonvulsants and Anti-Parkinsonian Drugs
  A. Anticonvulsants (Dilantin)
  B. Drugs for Petit Mal Epilepsy
  C. Drugs for Grand Mal and Psychomotor Epilepsy
  D. Anti-Parkinsonian Drugs
    1. Levodopa
    2. Anticholinergic Agents
    3. Amantadine

XIX. Endocrine System Drugs
  A. Pituitary Hormones
  B. Adrenal Corticosteroids
  C. Thyroid Agents
  D. Antithyroid Agents
  E. Antidiabetic Agents
    1. Insulin
    2. Oral Antidiabetic Agents

XX. Reproductive System Drugs
A. Classifications
1. Androgens
2. Estrogens
3. Progestins
4. Oral Contraceptives
   a. Progestin-only
   b. Norplant
   c. Progestasert
5. Drugs for Labor and Delivery
   a. Oxytocin
   b. Prostaglandin E_2
   c. Ergonovin (prevention of postpartum hemorrhage)
   d. Ritodrine (inhibits uterine contractions in premature labor)
   e. Magnesium Sulfate (Preeclampsia and Eclampsia)
6. Infertility Drugs
   a. Clomiphene Citrate
   b. Menotropins
   c. Chorionic Gonadotropin

XXI. Cardiovascular Drugs
A. Classifications
1. Cardiac Glycosides (Digitalis)
2. Antiarrhythmic Agents
   a. Adrenergic Blockers
   b. Calcium Blockers
   c. Disopyramide
   d. Lidocaine
   e. Procainamide
   f. Quinidine
3. Antihypertensives
   a. Beta-Adrenergic and Calcium Blockers
   b. Methyldopa
   c. Hydralazine
   d. ACE Inhibitors
4. Coronary Vasodilators - Treatment of Angina (Nitroglycerin)
5. Antilipemic Agents
6. Vasoconstrictors
7. Anticoagulants
   a. Coumarin derivatives
   b. Heparin
8. Platelet Inhibitor Therapy
   a. Persantine
   b. Aspirin

XXII. Respiratory System Drugs and Antihistamines
   A. Oxygen
   B. Respiratory Stimulants
      1. Caffeine citrate
      2. Theophylline
      3. Carbon Dioxide Inhalations
   C. Bronchodilators
      1. Sympathomimetics
      2. Parasympatholytics
      3. Xanthines
   D. Corticosteroids (relieves inflammation)
   E. Asthma Prophylaxis
   F. Mucolytics and Expectorants
   G Antitussives
   H. Antihistamines
   I. Decongestants

XXIII. Preoperative Medications
   A. Anticholinergics
   B. Antiemetics
   C. Sedative and Sedative Hypnotic
   D. Opioids

XXIV. Local Anesthetics
   A. Infiltration Anesthesia
   B. Direct Topical Anesthesia
   C. Peripheral Nerve Block
   D. Spinal Anesthesia
   E. Epidural Anesthesia

References for Pharmacology

Saunders Drug Handbook for Health Professions
       Kizior, BS, RPH and Barbara B. Hodgson, RN
       W. B. Saunders

Health Professionals Drug Guide 2004
       Shannon, Margaret T. et al.
       Prentice Hall. Upper Saddle River, New Jersey

The MERCK MANUAL of Diagnosis and Therapy
       Published by: Merck and Co., Inc.
       Rathway, NJ

American Medical Association Encyclopedia of Medicine
       Published by: AMA
       Chicago, IL

Taber's Cyclopedic Medical Dictionary
       Published by: F. A. Davis Company
       Philadelphia, PA

Boyd's Introduction to the Study of Disease
       Published by: Lea and Febiger
       Philadelphia, PA

Pathology for the Health-Related Professions
       Published by: W. B. Saunders Company
       Philadelphia, PA

Mosby's Medica, Nursing, and Allied Health Dictionary
       Published by: Mosby
       St. Louis, MO

STATISTICS

GENERAL

I. Statistical Process
  A. Definition of statistics
  B. Collection of data
  C. Organization of data
  D. Analysis of data
    1. Health facts stated numerically

II. Uses of Health Statistics
  A. To compare current performance with past
  B. To plan for the future
  C. To rate current performance
  D. To disburse funds
  E. To accredit and/or license facilities and programs

III. Users of Health Statistics
  A. Internal management of institution
    1. Collection of data to justify additions or closings
    2. Administrative Staff
    3. Medical Staff
      a. compare medical performance
      b. research
      c. educational purposes
    4. Allied Health Professional Staff
      a. rate and compare performance of ancillary units
      b. utilization review activities
      c. research
      d. educational purposes
      e. quality assurance studies.
  B. Health Agencies
    1. Federal
      a. National Center for Health Statistics
      b. Public Health Service
      c. Department of Health and Human Services (CMS)
    2. International Agencies
      a. International Red Cross
      b. WHO
    3. State Agencies
      a. Departments of Public Health
      b. Statewide planning agencies
  C. Accrediting and/or Approval Agencies
    1. Joint Commission on Accreditation of Health Organizations
    2. American Osteopathic Association (AOA)
    3. Department of Health and Human Services (CMS)
    4. American College of Surgeons (ACS) (Cancer Program accreditation)

IV. Internal Sources of Health Statistics
A. Primary
1. Original Health Record
2. Census Data
3. Vital Statistics
    a. birth certificates
    b. death certificates
    c. fetal death certificates
B. Secondary obtained from primary sources
1. Discharge Analysis Data
2. Departmental/Service Statistical Reports
3. Monthly/Annual Statistical Reports

V. External Sources of Health Statistics
A. Centers for Disease Control (CDC)
B. National Center for Health Statistics (NCHS)
C. Agency for Healthcare Research and Quality (AHRQ)

VI. Who Maintains Health Statistics?
A. Facilities
1. short-term hospital (ALOS less than 30 days)
2. long-term hospital (ALOS more than 30 days)
3. nursing Homes
4. ambulatory care facilities
    a. health clinics
    b. industrial/labor union clinics
    c. health department clinics
    d. HMOs
    e. ambulatory surgery facilities
B. Medical Staff Units
C. Other
1. school health programs
2. cancer programs
3. alcoholism/drug abuse programs
4. home care
5. hospice

VII. Uniform Reporting
A. Definition (Need consensus among those collecting statistical data as to what each item means)
B. Uniform Hospital Discharge Data Set (UHDDS) (Purpose is to satisfy need for uniform terms.)
C. Glossary of Health Care Terms - AHIMA (Used to define terms not included in descriptions for requested statistics)
D. Uniform Ambulatory Medical Care Minimum Data Set (MDS)
E. Long-Term Care Minimum Data Set Recommended by NCVHS (MDS)
F. CMS Long Term Care Requirements (MDS)

VIII. Data Collection
A. Retrospective
B. Concurrent

RETROSPECTIVE USE OF STATISTICAL DATA

I. **Monthly and Annual Reports from Discharge Data** (computed at local, state and national levels)
   A. Computation of percentages
   B. Computation of rates
      1. number of occurrences divided by possible occurrences
   C. Ratio
      1. an expression of comparison between 2 numbers
      2. usually written as one number before the other with a colon in between
      3. may be expressed as a fraction, decimal, quotient or proportion
      4. ratio converted to percentage can be called rate
   D. Reports
      1. monthly
      2. quarterly
      3. annually
   E. Common Hospital Rates and Percentages
      1. Death Rates (Mortality)
         a. Hospital Death Rate
            i. Gross
            ii. Net
            iii. Newborn
            iv. Fetal
         b. Postoperative Death Rate
         c. Maternal
      2. Autopsy Rate
         a. Gross
         b. Net
         c. Hospital
         d. Newborn
         e. Fetal
      3. Length of Stay
         a. Length of Stay
         b. Total Length of Stay
         c. Average Length of Stay (Average Stay) (ALOS) (LOS)
   F. Hospital Infection Rates
      1. nosocomial
      2. post-operative
   G. Consultation Rates
   H. Case Mix statistics
      1. case mix index
   I. Ambulatory Care statistics

CONCURRENT USE OF STATISTICS DATA

I. Inpatient Census (unit and hospital)
A. Census
   1. Census taking time
B. Daily Census
   1. Census plus number admitted and discharged same day
C. Inpatient/Resident/Service Day
D. Total Inpatient/Resident Service Days
E. Average Daily Inpatient/Resident Census (Average Daily Census)
F. Inpatient Bed Occupancy Rate (Percentage of Occupancy)
G. Bed Turnover Rate

MEASURES OF CENTRAL TENDENCY AND VARIATION

I. Measures of Central Tendency
A. Mean (average)
B. Median (midpoint)
C. Mode

II. Measures of Variation
A. Range
B. Variance
C. Standard Deviation

III. Measures of Dispersion
A. Range

IV. Tests of Significance
A. Chi Square
B. Type I error
C. Type II error

V. Normal Distribution
A. Bell-shaped curve

PRESENTATION OF DATA

I. Types of data
    A. Nominal data
    B. Ordinal data
    C. Discrete data
    D. Continuous data

II. Tables
    A. Constructing a Table
        1. Columns
        2. Rows
        3. Labels
    B. Frequency Distribution Tables
        1. Grouping data into classes
            a. rules for classes
                i. five to fifteen classes
                ii. small and largest figures represented
                iii. each item fits into one class only
                iv. classes should cover equal ranges of values

III. Graphs
    A. Construction
        1. Horizontal axis (independent variable)
        2. Vertical axis (dependent variable)
    B. Types of Graphs
        1. Bar Graph
        2. Histogram
        3. Line Graph
        4. Pie Graph
        5. Control
        6. Cause effect diagrams
        7. Pareto
        8. Run
        9. Scatter diagram
        10. Frequency polygon

IV. Statistical Software
    A. Spreadsheets (Excel)
    B. Statistical (SPSS or SAS)

VITAL RECORDS AND STATISTICS

I. Vital Records
   A. Birth Certificates (The physician is responsible for completion of certificates.)
   B. Death Certificates
   C. Fetal Death Certificates
   D. Definitions for Reporting Reproductive Health Statistics
      1. Fetal Death
      2. Induced Termination of Pregnancy
      3. Live Birth
         a. low birth weight neonate
         b. preterm neonate
         c. term neonate
         d. post term neonate

II. National Vital Statistics System (NVSS)
   A. Data collected from birth and death certificates
   B. Local Registrar or Vital Statistics Office
   C. State Registrar (source of certified copies)
   D. National Center for Health Statistics
   E. World Health Organization

III. Community or Population Based Statistics
   A. Mortality Rates
      1. neonatal
      2. post-neonatal
      3. infant
   B. Birth rates
   C. Other rates
      1. crude death rate
      2. cause-specific death rate
      3. case fatality
      4. proportionate mortality
      5. maternal mortality rate
   D. Measures of Morbidity
      1. Prevalence
      2. Incidence

RESEARCH STUDIES

I. Research
- A. Evaluation
    1. Steps in Research Process
    2. Review of Literature
    3. Explanation of Limitations of Study
    4. Sample Size and Type
    5. Appropriateness of Statistical Tests
    6. Reliability and Validity of Results
- B. Steps in Research
    1. Identify Topic
    2. Review of Literature
    3. Research Hypothesis Stated
    4. Research Design and Method
        a. select data gathering methods, techniques and instruments
        b. develop instruments
        c. data analysis plan
    5. Pilot Study
    6. Data Gathering and Analysis
    7. Report/Publication

References for Statistics

Health Information: Management of a Strategic Resource, 2nd Edition,
Abdelhak, et al.
W.B. Saunders

Basic Allied Health Statistics and Analysis
Gerda Koch
Delmar Learning

Basic Healthcare Statistics for HIM Professionals
Karen Garrett Youmans
AHIMA

Quality and Performance Improvement in Healthcare 2nd Edition.
Patricia Shaw, MEd, RHIA
AHIMA

Health Information Management Technology, An Applied Approach
Johns, Merida, et al.
AHIMA

Health Information Management: Concepts, Principles and Practices
LaTour, Kathleen, et al.
AHIMA

QUALITY IMPROVEMENT

I. Components Of A Hospital: Quality Management Program
   A. Quality improvement and performance
   B. Utilization management
   C. Risk management
   D. Credentialing
   E. Risk management

II. Quality Management
   A. Joint Commission (JCAHO)
      1. improving organizational performance
      2. management of information
   B. Major Legislation Relevant to Clinical Quality Management
      (Refer to LaTour and Eichenwald, 2002)

1	1965	PL 89-97	health coverage for citizens 65 and older
2.	1972	PL 92-603	PPSROs established
3.	1982	TEFRA	PROs and the PPS established
4.	1983	PL 98-21	PPS for Medicare established
5.	1985	COBRA	Denial of payment for substandard care authorized
6.	1986	PL 99-509	PROs required to report substandard care to licensing and certifying boards
7.	1986	PL 99-660	Health Care Quality Improvement Act
8.	1989	PL 101-239	Agency for Health Care Policy and Research created
9.	1990	PL 101-508	PROs required to inform licensing bodies of physician sanctions
10	1996	PL 104 181	Health Insurance Portability and Accountability Act

   C. Process of Quality improvement
      1. identify an opportunity
      2. involve a team
      3. initiate the collection of data
      4. implement improvement ideas
      5. evaluate progress
   D. Q. I. data tools
      1. Pareto charts
      2. flow charts
      3. cause and effect (fishbone) diagrams
      4. decision matrix
      5. histogram
      6. run charts
      7. scatter diagrams
      8. brainstorming
      9. nominal group technique
      10. customer satisfaction surveys
      11. decision matrix
      12. check sheet
      13. PDCA method (Plan Do Check Act)
   E. Q. I. components
      1. indicators/thresholds/aspects of care
      2. occurrence/generic screens
      3. sentinel events-Root Cause Analyses (RCAs)

F. Implementing QI
    1. create a quality strategy
    2. identify internal and external customers and their needs
    3. incorporate QI principles into departmental training programs
    4. develop a spirit of employee ownership
    5. develop teamwork within your department
    6. encourage a quality suggestion system
    7. establish a complaint tracking system
    8. conduct quality audits
    9. monitor the vital signs of quality efforts
    10. recognize employee quality efforts
    11. develop improvement teams

III. Utilization Management
A. History and legislation
    1. Title XVIII - Title XIX (1965)
B. Utilization program
    1. U. R. plan
    2. U. R. committee
C. Physician Advisor - PA (physician assistant)
D. Reviews (pre-established objective screening criteria is used)
    1. preadmission review
        a. review prior admission to determine if procedures and reason for admission os appropriate and necessary
    2. admission review
        a. determine if admission is medically necessary and appropriate
        b. length-of-stay assignments
    3. continued stay review
        a. review for continued medical necessity and appropriateness
    4. criteria
        a. generic criteria
        b. intensity of service/severity of illness (IS/SI)
    5. discharge review
        a. review at discharge to determine if the patient meets discharge screens
    6. retrospective review
        a. done for
            i.   evaluation of quality issues
            ii. costs and day outliers
            iii. utilization and appropriateness of admissions and resources
E. Discharge Planning (Should start before admission if possible)

IV. Credentialing

> **Credentialing**
>
> *Credentialing is the review, verification and evaluation of key factors that determine an individual's ability to carry out certain patient care activities. Additionally, it ensures the competency of the health care providers to include competency-based performance evaluation of non-physicians*

  A. Clinical privileges
    1. authorization granted by the governing body to a practitioner
    2. specifies exact patient care services that can be practiced within defined limits
    3. based on individual license, education, training, experience, competence health status and judgment
  B. Process of credentialing
    1. initial appointment to medical staff
    2. initial delineation and granting of clinical privileges
    3. periodic re-appointment to the medical staff (at least every two years)
    4. periodic renewal or revision of clinical privileges

V. Risk Management

> **Risk Management**
>
> *Risk management is an insurance and quality control related discipline comprising activities designed to minimize adverse effects of loss upon a health care organization's human, physical and financial assets through identification and assessment of loss potential loss, loss prevention and reduction, loss funding and risk financing and claim control.*

  A. Risk management program
    1. objectives
      a. create and maintain a safe healthy environment and enhance the quality of care
      b. minimize risk of medical or accidental injuries and losses
      c. provide cost-effective techniques to ensure against financial loss
    2. purpose
      a. identify, analyze, evaluate and eliminate and/or reduce all possible risks to patients, visitors and staff
    3. Components
      a. risk identification
      b risk control
      c. risk financing
    4. risk management committee
  B. Potential compensable events (PCE's)
  C. Risk evaluation and control

VI. Diagnostic Related Groups (DRGS)

  A. prospective payment system (PPS)
  B. case-mix management
    1. day outliers
    2. cost outliers
    3. discharges/transfers
  C. Prospective Payment Assessment Commission (PROPAC)
  D. Ambulatory patient groups
  E. Quality Improvement Organizations (QIOs) previously known as Peer-Review Organizations (PRO's)
  F. Resource-Based Relative Value System (RBRVS)

VII. Severity-refined DRGs (SRDRGs)
A. DRG re-classification
B. Atypical cases of DRGs
C. SDRG Diagnoses no longer CCs
D. SDRG Diagnoses now CCs

VIII. Critical Pathways
A. Critical paths and QI
B. Critical paths and practice parameters

IX. Clinical Pertinence
A. Difference between "critical paths" and clinical pertinence
B. Role and responsibility of the HI professional in both functions

QUALITY IMPROVEMENT AND PERFORMANCE MANAGEMENT SYLLABUS

QUALITY IMPROVEMENT AND PERFORMANCE
(Written by the Quality Improvement section of the AHIMA for educational purposes)

I. Early Efforts to Evaluate Medical Care
A. Assurance that the medical care provided was of high quality and was indirectly controlled through licensure of health care practitioners, granting of medical staff privileges and peer review mechanisms.
B. American College of Surgeons developed a voluntary accreditation program called the Hospital Standardization Program.
C. The Minimum Standard adopted in 1919 established professional support structures and evolved into what is now known as the Joint commission on Accreditation of Healthcare Organizations (JCAHO).

II. JCAHO Influence
A. JCAHO was a forerunner in evaluating medical care from a quality standpoint.
B. 1952 - JCAHO was formed as an outgrowth of the American College of Surgeons.
C. 1972 - JCAHO established a requirement for medical audits and a retrospective outcome-oriented methodology called the Performance Evaluation Procedure (PEP).
D. 1975 - A Quality of Professional Services standard was included in the Accreditation Manual for Hospital (AMH) and required hospitals to demonstrate the quality of patient care.
E. 1979 - JCAHO revised the approach to quality assurance by focusing on areas of problem resolution.

F. 1985 - A specific "Quality Assurance" chapter was included in the AMH.
 1. The problem-focused approach was replaced by a systematic monitoring and evaluation system to evaluate quality and appropriateness of care, pursue improvement of patient care, resolve identified problems and show the effectiveness of problem resolution.
 2. The process began with the identification of Care, Important Aspects of Care (high volume, high risk and problem prone activities).
 3. A ten-step process was introduced.
 4. Five monitoring activities were required and include
   a. Blood Usage Review
   b. Drug Usage Review
   c. Medical Record Review
   d. Pharmacy and Therapeutics Review
   e. Surgical Case Review
G. 1986 - A new developmental project entitled the "Agenda for Change" was begun. The intent was to shift accreditation emphasis from review of structure to process and outcome.
H. The first phase of a two-phase transition from standards organized around departments/services or structures to those organized around functions most critical to patient care.
 1. The word "quality" has changed to "performance".
 2. The *Cycle for Improving Performance* was established as a scientific model for making health care processes and outcomes better.
 3. The performance improvement cycle components are connected by actions of managers, physicians, clinicians, trustees and support staff who design, measure, assess and improve their work processes.
 4. The dimensions of performance are the characteristics of what is done and how it is done.
 5. JCAHO implemented the *Indicator Monitoring System* to provide a reference database comparison and feedback to the hospitals for evaluation of trends and comparison of performance.

III. Landmark Decisions
 A. Darling vs. Charleston Community Hospital
    A hospital must assume certain responsibilities for care of the patient.
 B. Gonzales vs. Nork and Mercy Hospital
    The hospital is negligent if it knew or had reason to know of a surgeon's incompetence.
 C. Johnson vs. Misericordia Hospital
    The hospital owes a duty to its patients in the selection of its medical staff and in granting privileges.

IV. Other Influences
  A. 1965 - Social Security Amendment Title XVIII (Medicare) and Title (XIX) programs were established.
  B. 1967 - Medicare Conditions of Participation
     Established and were revised in 1986 to include the quality assurance standard.
  C. 1983 - Peer Review Organizations (PROs)
     Established to provide review of health care services rendered to federally-funded patients.
  D. 1986 - Health Care Quality Improvement Act
     Federal laws that provided peer review protection and limited immunity for peer review activities.
     1. National Practitioner Data Bank was established as a central data bank to provide information on physician's and other health care practitioner's incompetence or improper professional conduct.

V. External Pressures for quality
  A. 1970-1980's - public's increased concern about inflation and rising cost of health care.
  B. 1990's - Managed care contracts have created competitive pressures among healthcare institutions. Physicians and hospitals agree to predetermined fees in exchange for network participation and agree to comply with quality standards, utilization management practices and provide outcome data.

VI. Internal Pressures for Quality
  A. New internal incentive for quality improvement by hospitals.
  B. Economic constraints from external pressures have placed an increasing emphasis on productivity and cost-efficiency.

VII. Components of a Hospital-Wide Quality program. Closely related and efficiently conduced in a collaborative, integrated program.
  A. Quality Improvement and Performance
  B. Utilization Management
  C. Credentialing
  D. Risk Management

VIII. Move from Quality Assurance to Quality Improvement
  A. Quality Assurance (Designed to monitor and evaluate quality issues prospectively, concurrently or retrospectively.)
     1. Three approaches
        a. structure (timeliness and appropriateness of care)
        b. process (accuracy of functions, activities, events or occurrence)
        c. outcome (end result of care)
     2. Criteria were established
        Predetermined elements of health care against which the aspects of quality of medical service may be compared.
     3. Priorities were established
        Predetermined elements of health care against which the aspects of quality of medical service may be compared.
     4. Evaluation of the problem(s) was done by
        a. identifying the site
        b. identifying the responsible party
        c. identifying the nature of the problem

5. Identified who and what needs to change, who is responsible for initiating the change and when the correction is to be completed.
6. Conclusions, recommendations and actions were established and implemented.
B. Quality Improvement - a process for encompassing the same basic concepts of Quality Assurance.
1. Leadership driven
2. Employee involvement
3. Enhances quality
C. Six key elements that distinguish QA from QI
1. A focus on process, not on people
2. Quality is defined as meeting the needs of the customer
3. Improving quality to reduce cost
4. Building quality into the process
5. Using a scientific approach to problem solving, structured tools and statistical process control methods and multidisciplinary teams
6. Approaching quality as a management strategy
D. Three basic components in defining a process
1. Suppliers and supplier inputs
2. Operation of the process
3. Customers and customer outputs
E. Organizations need to manage their quality through a strategy of continuous improvement.
F. Process management - results occur because of the way in which the process has evolved. To change the results, one must actively influence change in the process system or processes must be done to reduce variation from common causes.
G. Continuous quality improvement touches all parts of the organization and changes have to occur for it to work. The culture, the people, the systems, and the partnerships are the key to change.
H. Three quality themes are woven into the quality improvement process
1. clinical excellence
2. customer service
3. leadership
I. "Do It Right the first Time"

IX. Quality Management Components of the 1994-1995 health care reform proposals
A. National effort to measure health care performance
B. Development and dissemination of clinical practice guidelines
C. Managed Competition
Purchasers of comprehensive health services (largely employers, small employer coalitions and the government) will choose only those health plans which meet high quality, low cost criteria.

X. Measuring/Managing the Quality of Health Plan Performance

A. Late 1980's - Managed care organizations began to develop measures of quality and performance. Purchasers of health care services began to ask, *"How can purchasers understand what 'value' their health care dollar is purchasing and how can they hold a health plan 'accountable' for its performance?"*

B. Out of this effort came the Health Plan Employer Data and Information Set, (HEDIS), a core set of performance measures for managed care organizations. The National Committee for Quality Assurance (a professional association for managed care groups) took over the HEDIS project in 1991 and in November 1993 published HEDIS 2.0 (2nd revision). During 1994, the NCQA is working on a one-year pilot project involving 21 national or large regional managed care organizations to test the validity, reliability and usefulness of the HEDIS performance measures.

C. Managed care organizations began to release their own performance "report cards" in 1993.
   1. United Healthcare Corporation, Minneapolis, published their measurement results for quality of care, patient satisfaction, operating efficiency and cost reduction in the summer of 1993.
   2. U.S. Healthcare Inc., Blue Bell, PA, published 11 quality measures, including rates of childhood immunizations, cholesterol and mammography screenings and prenatal care in the fall of 1993.
   3. Kaiser Permanente, Oakland, CA, published their performance rates for 102 categories that include member satisfaction, child health, maternal care, cardiovascular disease and mental health in the fall of 1993.

XI. Quality Improvement Pioneers

A. Walter Shewhart - Original pioneer of QI and developed the statistical quality control (PDCA - Plan, Do, check, Act)

B. Edward Deming - His concepts were first implemented in Japan. His philosophy revolves around changing the current style of management to incorporate quality methods, techniques and tools into everyday work life. Identifies 14 points to follow for a successful QI program and Seven Deadly Diseases that create inconsistencies, make employees uncomfortable and fueled by profit.

C. Joseph M. Juran - Helped Japan implement quality concepts. Organizations need to find a universal approach to thinking about quality, "one which fits all functions, levels and all product lines." There are three basic quality oriented processes:
   1. Quality Planning
   2. Quality Control
   3. Quality Improvement

D. Philip Crosby - Established Four Quality Absolutes to improve quality in an organization. He also established a 14-Step Quality Improvement Program.

E. Brian Joiner - a proponent of Deming's philosophies and believes that quality improvement starts at the top and works its way down to the employees. He developed the Joiner Triangle with the three basic elements of Quality, Scientific approach and All-in-one Team.

XII. Quality Improvement Tools
   A. Brainstorming
   B. Customer Satisfaction Survey
   C. Flow Chart
   D. Cause and Effect Diagram
   E. Check Sheet
   F. Decision Matrix
   G. Pareto Chart
   H. Histogram
   I. Run Chart
   J. Scatter Diagram
   K. Nominal Group Technique

UTILIZATION MANAGEMENT

I. Utilization Management - A review of medical appropriateness and analysis of the efficiency in providing necessary services in the most cost-effective manner.
   A. Evaluates the level of care required
   B. Assesses alternate health care options
   C. Eliminates over-utilization, under-utilization and inefficient scheduling of services.

II. History
   A. 1950s - Allegheny County Medical Society - guidelines and the first review plan focusing on quality and cost of medical care were developed.
   B. Hospital Utilization Project (HUP) was formed to provide data support and consulting services for utilization review (UR) in Pennsylvania.
   C. 1965 - UR first became mandatory with the passage of Medicare (Title XVIII) of the Social Security Act.
   D. 1972 - Public Law 92-603 - Required concurrent review for Medicare and Medicaid patients.
   E. The Professional Standards Review Organization (PSRO) - a non-profit organization to perform professional reviews and evaluate patient care services for necessity, quality and cost-effectiveness. Required extended stay review for hospitals and long term care patients.
   F. 1977 - UR Act - Anti-Fraud and Abuse regulations for Medicare and Medicaid with continued stay as the main emphasis.
   G. 1982 - Peer Review Improvement Act - Redesigned the PSRO program and established the Peer Review Organization (PRO). Preadmission/Admission review for medical necessity and appropriateness of admissions was begun.
   H. 1982 - Tax Equity and Fiscal Responsibility Act (TEFRA)
       Prospective Payment System (PPS) changed the cost based payment system for Medicare and Medicaid to a Diagnosis Related Group (DRG) based reimbursement system.
   I. 1986 - Medicare Conditions of Participation was revised and included the Quality Assurance requirements.
   J. 1993 - PROs implemented the fourth Scope of Work under the Health Care quality Improvement Initiative (HQ+CQII) and will be a data-driven approach to monitoring care and outcomes.

III. JCAHO Utilization Review Requirement
A. Required by JCAHO since the early 1970s
B. 1980 - a separate UR standard required the hospitals to demonstrate appropriate allocation of its resources through an effective utilization review program.

IV. Utilization Management Plan is required and includes
A. Purpose
B. Lines of authority
C. Committee organization, responsibilities and function
D. Reporting mechanism
E. Administrative support
F. Relationship to other quality improvement activities
G. Procedure for updating the plan

V. The Utilization Management Program must be integrated with other data requirements to ensure that quality data are maintained and that each data element is collected only once.

VI. Utilization Review Process
A. Re-established objective screening criteria is used.
B. Preadmission review - Review prior to admission to determine if procedure and reason for potential admission is appropriate and necessary in an acute setting.
C. Admission review - Review to determine if the admission is medically necessary
D. Continued Stay Review - Review for continued medical necessity and appropriateness.
E. Discharge Review - Review at discharge to determine if the patient meets discharge screens.
F. Retrospective Review - Review done by the PRO for evaluation of quality issues, cost, day outliers and utilization and appropriateness of admissions and resources.

VII. Managed Care
A. Because it is evolving, managed care embraces a variety of existing and developing structures. It may be defined as
   1. Systems that integrate the financing and delivery of appropriate health care services to covered individuals through arrangements for comprehensive services with providers selected explicitly
   2. Formal, ongoing programs of quality improvement and utilization management
   3. Financial incentives for health plan enrollees to use providers and procedures associated with the plan
B. Case Management is a method of ensuring coordination and continuity of care during a patient's episode of illness. Case management is an interdisciplinary process to assess, plan and provide patient services. This process includes assessing and prioritizing a person's health care needs.
   1. Developing a plan of care that addresses the need in a cost-effective manner
   2. Identifying, arranging and coordinating the services
   3. Monitoring the patient's condition and responses to services
   4. Reassessing the person's needs on a regular basis

C. Hospital-Based Case Management is usually part of a broad, multi-disciplinary effort to coordinate patient care activities. Activities that might be included in the hospital's managed care strategy include:
1. Patient Care Coordination throughout the hospitalization
2. Patient Care Coordination throughout the entire episode of care
3. Clinical paths
4. Pre-admission programs
5. Quality/Cost Data Analysis
6. Concurrent Monitors of Resource Use
7. Third Party Payer contracting
8. Efficiency/Effectiveness Education for Physicians and Staff
D. Payer-Based Case management: Patient Care Coordination throughout the entire episode of care. The case management activities of payers focus on moving patients through the system through effective use of health care resources. The functions of payer-based case management include:
1. Ongoing data analysis
2. Collaboration with physicians, patients/families and other healthcare professionals
3. Ongoing oversight of the effectiveness of the health care delivery process

VIII. Managed Care
A. Because it is evolving, managed care embraces a variety of existing and developing structures. It may be defined as
1. Systems that integrate the financing and delivery of appropriate health care services to covered individuals through arrangements for comprehensive services with providers selected explicitly
2. Formal, ongoing programs of quality improvement and utilization management
3. Financial incentives for health plan enrollees to use providers and procedures associated with the plan
B. Case Management is a method of ensuring coordination and continuity of care during a patient's episode of illness. Case management is an interdisciplinary process to assess, plan and provide patient services. This process includes
1. Assessing and prioritizing a person's health care needs
2. Developing a plan of care that addresses the need in a cost-effective manner
3. Identifying, arranging and coordinating the services
4. Monitoring the patient's condition and responses to services
5. Reassessing the person's needs on a regular basis
C. Hospital-Based Case Management is usually part of a broad, multidisciplinary effort to coordinate patient care activities. Activities that might be included in the hospital's managed care strategy include
1. Patient Care coordination throughout the hospitalization
2. Patient Care Coordination throughout the entire episode of care
3. Clinical paths
4. Pre-admission programs
5. Quality/Cost data analysis
6. Concurrent monitors of resource use
7. Third party payer contracting
8. Efficiency/effectiveness education for physicians and staff
D. Payer-Based Case Management: Patient Care Coordination throughout the entire episode of care

E. The case management activities of payers focus on moving patients through the system through effective use the health care resources. The functions of payer-based case management may include:
1. Ongoing data analysis
2. Collaboration with physicians, patients/families and other healthcare professionals
3. Ongoing oversight of the effectiveness of the health care delivery process

CREDENTIALING

I. Credentialing has become very important to hospitals to ensure quality care is being provides to patients.
A. Review, verification and evaluation of the key factors that determine an individual's ability to carry out certain patient care activities.
B. Clinical privileges - authorization granted by the governing body to a practitioner to provide specific patient care services within defined limits, based on individual license, education, training, experience, competence, health status and judgment.
C. Key processes of Credentialing
1. Initial appointment to the medical staff
2. Initial delineation and granting of clinical privileges
3. Periodic re-appointment to the medical staff
4. Periodic renewal Periodic renewal or revision of clinical privileges
D. Hospitals must query the National Practitioner Data bank based on the Healthcare Quality Improvement Act.
E. Also required for granting of medical staff membership
1. Previously successful or currently pending challenges to licensure or registration
2. Voluntary relinquishment of licensure or registration
3. Voluntary or involuntary termination of medical staff membership
4. Voluntary or involuntary limitation, reduction or loss of clinical privileges at another facility
5. Departmental and peer recommendations
6. Participation in continuing education

II. Health plan credentialing activities

III. Credentialing activities in non-hospital provider settings.

IV. Ensuring the competency of health care providers to include competency-based performance evaluation of non-physicians.

RISK MANAGEMENT

I. **Health care risk management is an insurance and quality control-related discipline comprising activities designed to minimize adverse effects of loss upon a health care organization's human, physical and financial assets through identification and assessment of loss potential, loss prevention and reduction, loss funding and risk financing and claim control.**

II. **In the 1970's hospital-based risk management programs were developed based on the malpractice crisis.**
   A. Risk Financing
   B. Loss prevention and control
   C. Developed to combat high premium costs
   D. Attempted to reduce the frequency and severity of losses

III. **Three basic objectives of a Risk Management program**
   A. To create and maintain a safe, healthy environment and enhance the quality of care
   B. To minimize risk of medical or accidental injuries and losses
   C. To provide cost-effective techniques to insure against financial loss

IV. **An effective risk management program incorporates the identification, analysis, evaluation and elimination or reduction of possible risks to patients, visitors and employees.**

V. **Components of a Risk Management Program**
   A. Risk identification - areas of potential or existing loss.
   B. Risk control - the loss prevention and control aspect were designed to control preventable risks and keep to a minimum the incidents for which the institution might be held liable.
   C. Risk financing - a plan for the following types of funds to cover losses are
      i.   self-insurance
      ii. insurance pools
      iii. commercial insurance.

VI. **Risk Management programs should be integrated with the facility's quality improvement program.**

References for Quality Assessment and Improvement

Quality Improvement Techniques for Medical Records
Cofer, J.I., and Greeley, H.P. (1996)
Opus Communications. Marblehead, MA

Health Information Technology: An Applied Approach
Johns, M. et. al. (2002)
AHIMA. Chicago, IL

Comprehensive Accreditation Manual for Hospital: The Official Handbook
Joint Commission on Accreditation of Healthcare Organizations
Oakbrook Terrace, IL

Health Information Management: Concepts Principles and Practices
LaTour, K. and Eichenwald, S. (2002)
AHIMA. Chicago, IL

Legal Aspects of Health Care Administration, 8th Edition
Pozgar, G.D. (1999)
Aspen. Gaithersburg, MD

Performance Improvement in Health Information Services
Rudman, W.J. (1997)
W.B. Saunders. Philadelphia. PA

Quality and Performance Improvement in Healthcare: A Tool for Programmed Learning, 2nd Edition
Shaw, Patricia. (2003)
AHIMA. Chicago, IL

Outcomes Management: Using Data for Decision Making
Spath, P.L., Smith, M.E., and Pelling, MH. (1995)
Brown, Spath and Associates. Forest Grove, OR

MEDICO-LEGAL ASPECTS

THE BASICS

I. Sources of Law
   A. Common law
1. originated in England
2. termed as "case law" (case decisions)
   a. decisions which follow these legal principles (case decisions) are called legal precedents

Legal Principle
stare decisis - *let the decision stand*

3. unwritten (non-statutory)
4. based on custom and tradition
   B. Statutory Law
1. laws created by state or federal legislatures
2. "written laws" (enacted laws by legislature)
   C. Administrative Law
1. the "rules and regulations" set forth by the state/federal governmental agencies
   D. The U.S./State Constitutions

II. OTHER LAWS
   A. Civil Law/Private Law
1. regulates private wrongs
2. involves monetary rewards for damages
3. does not deal with crimes
4. involves actions filed by one individual against another
   B. Criminal Law/Public Law
1. involves cases of public wrongs
2. crimes committed against society
3. crime (punishment applies)
4. legal action is brought forth by the state or federal governments against an individual(s)

III. LEGAL SYSTEM
   A. Federal
1. powers which affect the country as a whole and regulates issues between states
2. imposes taxes
3. addresses issues with foreign governments
   B. State
1. exercises powers in accordance with state laws and state constitution
2. protects the welfare, safety and health of the state constituents
   C. Local
1. authority over counties, cities, townships and villages
2. power to enact local laws
3. imposes taxes on property and goods
4. manages the school systems
5. elect local officials

IV. Branches of State/U.S. Government

> **Laws are made at:**
> - *State level: state legislature*
> - *Federal level: U.S. Congress*

A. Legislative Branch
   1. determines the needs for or changes in the laws
   2. consists of two houses
B. Executive Branch
   1. president of the U.S.
   2. enforces and administers the laws
   3. divided into departments and subdivided into agencies
      a. agencies have the power to administer and implement the legislation ("rules and regulations")
C. Judicial Branch
   1. Federal and State Courts
   2. responsible for administering justice
   3. applies the laws enacted by the legislative branch
   4. settles disputes between parties

V. Court System
A. Federal

> **Jurisdiction**
> - *authority or legal power to hear and decide cases*

   1. has jurisdiction over
      a. issues based on the U.S. Constitution
      b. federal laws
      c. treaties
      d. cases of maritime issues
B. Federal Courts
   1. Supreme Court of the U.S.

> **Supreme Court**
> - *tries lawsuits between 2 states*
> - *tries lawsuits involving ambassadors or counsel from foreign countries*
> - *may review decisions by the highest court of a state if constitutional question or federal law is involved*
> - *does not have to hear all cases from the state level; hears about 150 cases a year*
> - *has jurisdiction over the U.S. District Court*

      a. U.S. Court of Appeals
      b. U.S. District Court
      c. Other Specialty Courts
         i.   U.S. Claims Court
         ii. U.S. Court of International Trade
         iii. U.S. Tax Court
   2. U.S. Court of Appeals/Circuit Courts of Appeal
      a. may hear appeals from decisions of bankruptcy court and federal administrative agencies previously tried in U.S. District Court

3. U.S. District Court

> **U.S. District Court**
>
> *In civil cases:*
> - *plaintiff and defendant must be residents of different states*
> - *amount of money involved must be greater than $10,000*

    a. courts of general jurisdiction
    b. has original jurisdiction over cases involving
    c. divided by geographic regions
       1. bankruptcy, postal or banking laws, crimes involving federal laws, patents, trademarks, copyrights, crimes committed on high seas
    d. has power to hear and judge on criminal and civil cases

VI. State Courts
  A. State Supreme Court
  B. Appellate Courts

> **State Appellate Court/Courts of Appeals**
> - *hears only appeals from lower courts*
> - *no testimony of witnesses or exhibits*
> - *cases proceed on the basis of written briefs*
> - *presents oral arguments after briefs are submitted*
> - *reverses, modifies, affirms the decision*
> - *decides whether the trial judge applied law or instructed the jury correctly*

    1. looks to the record of events at a trial to determine if error in law or procedure occurred which would warrant reversal of the court decision
  C. Trial Courts

> **Duties Of Trial Court**
> - *helps to enforce the law*
> - *decides disputes*
> - *interprets statutes*
> - *supplies guidance in the current interpretation of the law*
> - *judge decides questions of law*
> - *jury decides questions of fact*
> - *jury renders a verdict*
> - *judge renders a judgment*

    1. conduct cases of criminal/civil matters
    2. initially hear a case and makes a judgment
    3. have responsibility for finding the facts in a case
  D. Municipal Courts

VII. Torts
A. Characteristics
1. defined as a civil wrong against an individual
2. may be classified as intentional or unintentional
3. an act that violates your private or personal rights
B. Types of Torts
1. Malpractice
a. any professional misconduct, improper discharge of professional duties or failure to meet the standard of a professional that resulted in harm to another
b. professional negligence
C. Intentional Torts
1. Assault and battery
a. assault: intentional act that is designed to make the victim fearful and produces reasonable apprehension of harm
b. battery: intentional touching of one person by another without the consent of the person being touched

> **EXAMPLE: Assault and Battery**
> *performing surgery on an individual without their consent*

2. False Imprisonment
a. the unlawful restraint of an individual against their will or the confining of an individual
b. does not require that there be physical force

> **EXAMPLE: False Imprisonment**
> *preventing a patient from leaving a health facility*

3. Defamation
a. injury of a person's reputation or character caused by willful, malicious and false statement of another made to a third party
b. libel
i. false or malicious writing intended to defame another person and is printed so that someone other than the defamed person will see it
c. slander
i. a false oral statement, made in the presence of a third person, that injures the character or reputation of another
D. Negligence

> **Negligence**
> *The standard of care that results in a tort (i.e. malpractice)*

1. the failure to exercise the standard of care that would be expected by a normally reasonable and prudent person in a particular set of circumstances
2. a civil or personal wrong distinguished from criminal conduct
3. omissions or commissions of an act
4. the most frequent basis for liability of health care professionals and hospitals is the negligent tort
5. elements that must be present for a plaintiff to recover damages caused by negligence
a. duty to care
b. breach of that duty
c. actual injury
d. causation/proximate cause

THE SPECIFICS

I. The Legal Procedure
  A. Parties in a lawsuit
    1. Defendant
      a. the party who is being sued
      b. the party defending or denying a claim in a lawsuit
    2. Plaintiff
      a. the party who brings a civil suit seeking damages or other legal action
      b. the party who begins an action of law
      c. the complaining party in an action
  B. Officers of the Court
    1. Judge
      a. chief member of a court
      b. elected or appointed
      c. ensures that both sides are treated fairly during a trial
      d. ensures the law is properly applied
    2. Clerk of Court
      a. responsible for court records
      b. keeps track of trial calendar
      c. issues various directives
        i. summons
        ii. subpoenas
      d. enters judgments and orders
      e. gives certified copies from records
      f. has charge of exhibits
    3. Bailiff
      a. court attendant who maintains order in the courtroom
      b. supervises or guards the jury
      c. attends to seating of witnesses
    4. Court Reporter
      a. records all proceedings on the courtroom
    5. Attorney
      a. person who has been formally trained and licensed by special examination to be a member of the legal profession
      b. qualified to give legal advice
      c. to act in legal formalities and negotiations
    6. Jury
      a. body of men and women selected and sworn in by a local court to try to determine any question of fact, according to the evidence given
  C. Documents Relating to a Lawsuit
    1. Subpoena
      a. court order requiring someone to appear in court to give testimony
      b. disregarding a subpoena can result in arrest
    2. Subpoena Duces Tecum
      a. court order that commands a person to come to court and produce whatever documents are named in the order

D. Legal Proceedings Before Trial
1. present case to attorney
2. attorney reviews case
3. attorney prepares complaint with the summons attached

Complaint
- *initial pleading in a lawsuit*
- *plaintiff alleges a cause of action*
- *asks that wrong done be remedied by the court*

Summons
- *the process by which an legal action begins*
- *defendant is notified that a legal action has been brought forth against him*
- *must respond*

---

4. defendant answers the complaint
5. if defendant fails to respond, he can be found liable by default
6. pretrial hearing
   a. discovery

Discovery
- *disclosure of facts and documents by one party at the request of the other*
- *used to prepared the case for trial*
- *facilitates out of court settlements*

---

   b. deposition

Deposition
- *sworn statement of fact*
- *made outside of court*
- *may be admitted as evidence in court*

---

   c. interrogatories

Interrogatories
- *written questions presented to a party or witness*
- *helps parties prepare for trial*
- *designed to gather information*

---

7. The Trial
   a. selection of jury
   b. attorney's opening statements
   c. questioning of witnesses
      i. direct examination
      ii. cross examination
      iii. redirect examination and re-cross examination
   d. evaluation of evidence and verdict by jury
   e. judge determines action to be taken based on jury's decision

II. Criminal Law
A. Crime
1. defined as a wrongful act against society punishable by the state
2. state is responsible to prosecute and bear expense of legal action against the defendant
B. The Law
1. involves cases of public wrong
2. crimes committed contrary to society's law
3. law relating to crime and punishment
4. legal action is filed by the state or by the U.S. against an individual
C. Other Aspects
1. defendant is the one who is accused of the crime
2. criminal charges may be brought about by
   a. indictment

Indictment
• *voted by the grand jury*
• *formal written accusation in accordance with the law*
• *charges a person named with a criminal act*

   b. filing of information

Filing Of Information
• *presented by a public officer instead of the grand jury*

   c. warrant or arrest of the person
   d. preliminary hearing
3. if sufficient evidence is presented, the defendant is bound over for trial
4. arraignment
   a. to call into court a person indicted for a crime
   b. read the indictment and instruct the defendant to plead guilty or not guilty

III. Non-Governmental Rule Making Bodies
A. Accreditation Agencies
1. JCAHO
2. CARF
B. Hospital and Health Care Associations
C. Governing Body/Governing Boards

IV. Patient's Rights
A. Patient's Bill of Rights
B. Ownership of record

CONFIDENTIALITY

I. Classification of Patient Information
    A. non-confidential information
    B. confidential information
    C. privileged information

> **Confidential Communications**
> - *information given in the belief that no disclosure will be made to another party*
> - *data of personal and private nature*
> - *statement made to an attorney, physician, or anyone else in a position of trust*

II. Confidentiality
    A. confidential and privileged communications
    B. elements of privileged communication

III. Non-confidential Information
    A. relates to the identification of a specific patient
    B. informational in nature
    C. considered to be common knowledge
    D. disclosure should be governed by written policy
    E. use caution when releasing

> **Non-Confidential Information:**
> ***May include but is not limited to***
> - *name of patient*
> - *age of the patient*
> - *verification of hospitalization*
> - *date of admission*
> - *date of discharge*

IV. Confidential Communications
    A. may include but is not limited to
        1. medical history
        2. social history
        3. diagnosis
        4. treatment
        5. medical and nursing notes
        6. discharge summary
    B. released only upon proper authorization for the release of information or by court order

V. Elements of Privileged Communications
    A. physician-patient relationship must exist
    B. information must be acquired through the physician-patient relationship
    C. information must relate to the TX and DX of the said patient

> **Privileged Communication**
> *Information received by special categories of people, who by law, cannot be forced to reveal such information in any legal proceeding without consent.*

VI. Privacy Act of 1974

A. Covers any record or record system maintained by an agency of the federal government with data identifiable to an individual including medical, education, financial etc., that can be retrieved by that identifier

B. The Act
1. allows an individual to know of his/her information being in the record system and what the information is to be used for and who has accessed the record
2. allows access to record
3. allows the individual to amend or correct the record
4. allows the individual to have a copy of his/her record
5. helps prevent the use beyond that which data was collected

VII. Ownership of the Medical Record

A. the physical property of the health care institution
B. content is the property of the patient
C. health care institution owns the medium on which the record is contained

---

Ownership of Record

- *patient can not take possession of original record*
- *patient has control over the information in the record, except where this limited by law or in circumstances where the health care institution must defend its interests or the best interests of the patient*

VIII. Patient Access to the Medical Record

A. Illinois law allows for patient access to the record after discharge

MEDICAL RECORD AND THE LAW

I. Consents

A. Types of Consents
1. expressed
2. implied
3. informed
4. implied by emergency

B. Informed Consent
1. informed, voluntary authorization for an act to be performed
   a. medical treatment
   b. disclosure of medical records
   c. surgical procedures
2. doctrine that identifies the physician's duty to explain the procedure to patients and to warn them of any material risks or dangers inherent in so that they can make intelligent and informed choices about whether or not to undergo the treatment
3. JCAHO requires "evidence of appropriate informed consent"
4. performing treatment on an individual without receiving his/her informed consent is assault and battery

C. Expressed Consent
1. consent given by direct words
2. written or oral
3. difficult to prove oral consent, most providers seek written consent

D. Implied Consent
    1. inferred from the patient's conduct
    2. presumed in certain emergencies unless provider has reason to believe the consent would be refused
E. Emergency Consent
    1. consent to emergency treatment belongs to the patient unless the patient is in immediate danger of death or loss of limb or is incapable of giving consent
    2. consent may be obtained over the telephone in an emergency situation
F. Who may consent?
    1. competent adults
    2. emancipated minors
        a. married
        b. self-supporting
        c. living independent from parents
    3. minors in exceptional circumstances (mental health treatment)
    4. Who consents for adults?
        a. competent adult
        b. guardian or other person authorized in the case of incompetent adult
        c. person with power of attorney
    5. Who consents for minors?
        a. parent
        b. legally appointed guardian
        c. custodian

II. Legal Aspects and Requirements of Consents for Specific Procedures
   A. Abortion
   B. Sterilization
   C. Artificial Insemination
   D. Experimentation
   E. Autopsies

SPECIAL RECORDS

I. Mental Health and Developmental Disabilities
   A. State statute
   B. What constitutes a valid authorization
   C. Confidential information
       1. release of
       2. refusal to authorize
       3. invalid authorization
       4. access by patient
       5. modifying the record
       6. documentation
   D. Therapist's personal notes
       1. issues of disclosure
       2. elements

E. Circumstances of releasing confidential information to/for
 1. other health care facilities
 2. transfer
 3. emergency
 4. patient's parent or guardian
 5. insurance companies
 6. financial concerns
 7. governmental agencies
 8. child abuse
 9. workmen's compensation
 10. firearms
 11. medical examiner
 12. social agencies
 13. news media
 14. attorneys
 15. legal proceedings
F. Privilege
 1. refusal
 2. waiver
G. Processing subpoenas
 1. legal effect
 2. court order
H. Retention requirements
 1. Re-disclosure
I. Definitions

II. Alcohol and Drug Abuse Records
A. Federal regulations
 1. relating to drug abuse
 2. relating to alcohol abuse
B. Exclusions
C. Permissible and non-permissible disclosures and communications
D. Components of authorizations
 1. components of valid authorizations
 2. who is authorized
 3. access/disclosures
 4. notice
 5. invalid authorizations
E. Circumstances of releasing confidential information to/for
 1. minors
 2. facility personnel
 3. other facilities
 4. emergency
 5. patient's family
 6. financial concerns
 7. insurance
 8. other
F. Vital statistics
G. Death
 1. release of information
H. FDA

I. Processing subpoenas
   1. legal effect
   2. court order
J. Research
K. Discontinued programs
L. Child abuse
M. Definitions

III. AIDS
A. General guidelines
   1. Records of patients infected with HIV should not be labeled to draw attention to it being different.
   2. It should be kept secure, if possible, with the other records.
   3. Caution should be exercised to avoid releasing information on HIV patients to employers or insurers.
   4. Hospitals should be careful not to place any reference to HIV on billing forms.
   5. Disease indexes and other reporting should use only numbers to identify patients, not names.
   6. Policies regarding confidentiality of HIV records should be made known to all employees and each should be required to sign a statement indicating they understand and will abide by all confidentiality rules.
   7. Information on HIV patients must not be released without clear and specific written authorization.
      a. Statements such as "any and all information" or "entire record" should never be sufficient to release HIV related information.
      b. Only information required to fulfill the purpose stated on authorization should be released.
B. HIV testing
   1. requirements
   2. exceptions
   3. notification
C. AIDS registry system
D. HIV Counseling and Testing Centers
E. AIDS and school systems

OTHER ISSUES

I. Record Retention

> **Record Retention**
>
> *Retains complete medical records of minors for the period of minority plus the applicable period of statute of limitations as prescribed by statute.*

A. AHA states that a facility retain basic information such as
   1. dates of admission and discharge
   2. names of responsible physician
   3. records of diagnoses and operations
   4. operative reports
   5. pathology reports
   6. discharge summaries
B. retention factors
   1. requirements imposed by law
   2. retention period that is recommend by outside agencies, licensing and accrediting agencies
   3. availability of storage space
   4. medium for storing records
   5. activity of records for continued patient care
   5. historical value
   6. research and education
C. AHIMA's Retention Guidelines

II. Computerized Health Record

A. advantages
   1. fast and accurate
   2. enormous capacity to store data
   3. reduction of paper work
   4. may become an economic necessity
   5. access to the patient record by multiple users
B. disadvantage
   1. confidentiality
   2. equipment failure
   3. questionable accuracy of input data
   4. unauthorized disclosure of information

Reference for Legal Issues

Health Information: Management of a Strategic Resource, 2nd Edition
  Abdelhak, M., et al. (2001)
  W.B. Sanders Company. Philadelphia, PA

Health Information Management Concepts, Principles, and Practice
  LaTour, K., and Eichenwald, S. (2002)
  American Health Information Management Association (AHIMA). Chicago, IL

Legal Aspects of Health Care Administration, 8th Edition
  Pozgar, G. D. (2003)
  Aspen Publications. Gaithersburg, MD

Medical Records and the Law, 3rd Edition
  Roach, W. H. (1998)
  Aspen Publications. Gaithersburg, MD

HEALTH INSURANCE PORTABILITY AND ACCOUNTABILITY ACT (HIPAA) 1996

I. Background - Original Legislation
The Health Insurance Portability and Accountability Act of 1996 (PL 104-191) is also known as the Kennedy-Kassebaum Act. The five objectives of this legislation were enacted to
A. Improve the portability and continuity of health insurance coverage
B. Promote the use of medical savings accounts
C. Combat waste, fraud and abuse in health insurance and health care delivery
D. Improve access to long-term care services and coverage
E. Simplify the administration of health insurance

II. Background - Legislative Amendments
A. Mental Health Parity Act
B. Newborns and Mothers Health Protection Act
C. Women's Health and Cancer Rights Act

III. Compliance Schedule/Timetable
A. 2002 *Transactions and Code Sets*
    all covered entities who did not file for an extension except small health plans
B. April 14, 2003 *Privacy*
    all covered entities except small health plans
C. April 16, 2003 *Transactions and Code Sets*
    all covered entities who have filed extensions must have started software and systems testing
D. October 16, 2003 *Transactions and Code Sets*
    all covered entities who filed for an extension and small health plans
    Medicare will only accept paper claims under limited circumstances
E. April 14, 2004 *Privacy*
    small health plans
F. July 30, 2004 *Employer Identifier Standard*
    all covered entities except small health plans
G. April 20, 2005 *Security*
    all covered entities except small health plans
H. August 1, 2005 *Employer Identifier Standard*
    small health plans
I. April 20, 2006 *Security*
    small health plans

IV. Enforcement of the Regulations
A. In states that have standards that substantially conform to or exceed these federal standards, or states that otherwise enforce the federal standards, state insurance regulators have primary enforcement authority for insurance carriers.
B. For those states that do not have such standards, CMS "directly" enforces HIPAA and the related amendments.

V. Privacy Rule- *Standards for Privacy of Individually Identifiable Health Information*

The Department of Health and Human Services (HHS) published the Privacy Rule on December 28, 2000 and adopted modifications of the Rule on August 14, 2002. This rule was enacted to ensure that the mandate for electronic transmission of private health information did not result in a loss of patient privacy.

VI. The Privacy Rule (45 CFR Part 160 and Subparts A and E of Part 164) provides for

  A. Three types of covered entities governed by the privacy rule
     1. Health Plans
     2. Heath Care Clearinghouses
     3. Health Care Providers who transmit health care information in electronic format
  B. Business Associates with whom the covered entities contract
  C. What the Privacy Rule Does
     1. The HIPAA Privacy Rule, for the first time, creates national standards to protect individuals' medical records and other personal health information [or protected health information (PHI)] because the rule
        a. gives patients more control over their health information
        b. sets boundaries on the use and release of health records
        c. establishes appropriate safeguards that health care providers and others must achieve to protect the privacy of health information
        d. holds violators accountable, with civil and criminal penalties that can be imposed if they violate patients' privacy rights
        e. strikes a balance when public responsibility supports disclosure of some forms of data (for example, to protect public health)
     2. For patients, it means being able to make informed choices when seeking care and reimbursement for care based on how personal health information may be used. The rule
        a. enables patients to find out how their information may be used and about certain disclosures of their information that have been made
        b. generally limits release of information to the minimum reasonably needed for the purpose of the disclosure
        c. generally gives patients the right to examine and obtain a copy of their own health records and request corrections
        d. empowers individuals to control certain uses and disclosures of their health information
  D. Activities required of providers or health plans under the rule
     1. Notifying patients about their privacy rights and how their information can be used
     2. Adopting and implementing privacy procedures for its practice, hospital or plan
     3. Training employees so that they understand the privacy procedures
     4. Designating an individual to be responsible for seeing that the privacy procedures are adopted and followed
     5. Securing patient records containing individually identifiable health information so that they are not readily available to those who do not need them
  E. Major modifications made to the privacy rule include
     1. Uses and disclosures for treatment, payment and health care operations
     2. Eliminating the requirement for the individual's consent for these activities
     3. The notice of privacy practices that covered entities must provide to patients
     4. Minimum necessary uses and disclosures
     5. Parents as the personal representatives of un-emancipated minors
     6. Uses and disclosures for research purposes
     7. Transition provisions, including business associate contracts
     8. Uses and disclosures for marketing purposes

F. Content Requirements for Consent to Use and Disclose Patient Specific Health Information to Carry Out Treatment and Payment of Health-Care Operations
   1. Consent must be in plain English
   2. Inform the individual that the information may be used and disclosed to carry out treatment, payment or healthcare operations
   3. Refer the individual to the notice of information practices
   4. Inform the individual of the right to review the notice before signing the consent
   5. State that the notice may change and that the individual has a right to receive a revised notice
   6. Inform the individual of the right to restrict use and disclosure of the information and the healthcare provider's option not to agree to the restriction
   7. State that the individual may revoke consent in writing except to the extent the healthcare provider has taken action in reliance thereon
   8. Be signed by the individual and dated
G. Exemptions from the consent requirement
   1. Public Interest and Benefit Activities
      a. When required by law (e.g., statute, regulation or court order)
      b. Public health activities
H. Administrative Requirements
   1. Privacy policies and procedures
   2. Privacy Personnel
   3. Workforce Training and Management
   4. Mitigation
   5. Data Safeguards
   6. Complaints
   7. Retaliation and Waiver
   8. Documentation and Record Retention

VII. Security Rule- Health Insurance Reform: Security Standards: Final Rule
45 CFR Parts 160, 162 and 164

> This rule is a subset of the privacy rule and is directed towards electronic health information. It is also tied to the transaction and code regulations of the administrative simplification section of HIPAA.

A. Three types of covered entities governed by the security rule
1. Health Plans
2. Heath Care Clearinghouses
3. Health Care Providers who transmit health care information in electronic format
B. System Vendors
C. General Administrative Requirements Part 160
1. Definitions
a. Electronic media
i. Electronic storage media
ii. Transmission media
iii. Electronic protected health information
iv. Individual
b. Organized health care arrangement
c. Protected health information
d. Use
D. Administrative Requirements Part 162-Authority cited
E. Security and Privacy Part 164-Authority cited
1. Definitions
a. Common control
b. Common ownership
c. Covered functions
d. Health care component
e. Hybrid entity
f. Plan sponsor
g. Required by law
2. Applicability
3. Organizational requirements
a. Health care component standard
b. Affiliated covered entities standard
c. Documentation standard
4. Security Standards for the Protection of Electronic Health Information
a. Applicability
b. Definitions
c. Security standards, general rule
d. Administrative safeguards
e. Physical safeguards
f. Technical safeguards
g. Organizational requirements
h. Policies and procedures and documentation requirements
i. Compliance dates for the initial implementation of the security standards

Appendix A to Subpart C of Part 164-Security Standards Matrix		
Standards	**Sections**	**Implementation Specifications** **(R) = Required** **(A) = Addressable**
Administrative Safeguards		
Security Management Process	164.308(a)(1)	Risk Analysis (R) Risk Management (R) Sanction Policy (R) Information System Activity Review (R)
Assigned Security Responsibility	164.308(a)(2)	(R)
Workforce Security	164.308(a)(3)	Authorization and/or Supervision (R) Workforce Clearance Procedure Termination Procedure (A)
Information Access Management	164.308(a)(4)	Isolating Healthcare Clearinghouse Function (R) Access Authorization (A) Access Establishment and Modification (A)
Security Awareness and Training	164.308(a)(5)	Security reminders (A) Protection from Malicious Software (A) Log-In Monitoring (A) Password Management (A)
Security Incident Procedures	164.308(a)(6)	Response and Reporting (R)
Contingency Plan	164.308(a)(7)	Data Back-up Plan (R) Disaster Recovery Plan (R) Emergency Mode Operation Plan (R) Testing and Revision Procedures (A) Application and Data Criticality Analysis (A)
Evaluation	164.308(a)(8)	(R)
Business Associate Contracts and Other Arrangement	164.308(b)(1)	Written Contract or Other Agreement (R)
Physical Safeguards		
Facility Access Controls	164.310(a)(1)	Contingency Operations (A) Facility Security Plan (A) Access Control and Validation Procedures (A) Maintenance Records (A)
Workstation Use	164.310(b)	(R)
Workstation Security	164.310(c)	(R)
Device and Media Controls	164.310(d)(1)	Disposal (R) Media Re-Use (R) Accountability (A) Data Backup and Storage (A)

Appendix A to Subpart C of Part 164-Security Standards Matrix (continued)		
Standards	**Sections**	**Implementation Specifications** **(R) = Required** **(A) = Addressable**
Technical Safeguards		
Access Control	164.312(a)(1)	Unique User Identification (R) Emergency Access Procedure (R) Automatic Logoff (A) Encryption and Decryption (A)
Audit Controls	164.312(b)	(R)
Integrity	164.312(c)(1)	Mechanisms to Authenticate Electronic Protected Health Information (A)
Person or Entity Authentication	164.312(d)	(R)
Transmission Security	164.312(e)(1)	Integrity Controls (A) Encryption (A)

References for HIPAA

Understanding the Health Insurance Portability and Accountability Act (HIPAA): A Volunteers in Health Care Guide
    Geller, S (2003)
    Volunteers in Health Care. Pawtucket, RI

Legal Aspects of Health Information Management
    McWay, Dana (2003)
    Thomson-Delmar Learning

Privacy and Confidentiality of Health Information
    Dennis, J. C. (2000)
    Jossey-Bass. San Francisco

U. S. Department of Health and Human Services (2001)
    HHS fact sheet: Protecting the privacy of patient's health information
    Retrieved August 25, 2002, from:
    http://www.hhs.gov/news/press/2002pres/privacy.html

Additional Web Sites:

    http://www.access.gpo.gov/su_docs/fedreg/a030220c.html

    http://library.ahima.org/xpedio/groups/secure/documents/government/bok1_016663.pdf

    http://www.cms.hhs.gov/hipaa/hipaa2/regulations/privacy/finalrule/privrulepd.pdf

    http://www.hhs.gov/ocr/privacysummary.rtf

JOINT COMMISSION ON ACCREDITATION OF HEALTH CARE ORGANIZATIONS
JCAHO

THE ORGANIZATION

I. **JCAHO**
   A. Private, non-profit (establishes guidelines and standards for operation and management of health care facilities)
      1. JCAHO plays a significant role in setting expectations for quality patient care which is reflected in the medical record.
   B. Develops standards by which health care facilities can evaluate themselves and be measured against.
   C. Standards
      1. based on premise that health care organizations exist to maximize people's health
      2. revised annually
      3. states outcomes; the standards don't prescribe how the outcomes are to be achieved, that is left to the facility
   D. Conducts surveys to determine if a health care facility meets the standards
   E. Accreditation by the JCAHO is an indicator that a health care facility has achieved a level of quality beyond the minimum requirements for licensure
      1. third party payors and the federal government use the JCAHO accreditation as a means of qualifying health care organizations for various programs or payment of services
         a. the Conditions for Participation (COP) in the Medicare Program are considered to be met (deemed status) if the facility has attained accreditation by the JCAHO
   F. Accreditation given for up to 3 years if a health care facility is found to be in compliance with the standards
      1. facilities are surveyed every 3 years
   G. JCAHO publishes accreditation manuals and conducts surveys for
      1. hospitals
      2. psychiatric facilities
      3. long-term care facilities
      4. substance abuse facilities
      5. home care facilities
      6. ambulatory care facilities
      7. organization-based pathology and clinical laboratory services
      8. mentally retarded and developmentally disabled
      9. hospice
      10. integrated delivery systems

Go to the JCAHO web page (JCAHO.org). In the "search" section type in "delinquency" and you will see a link for 2004 Decision Process and Decision Rules for Critical Access Hospitals

---

H. In 1994, JCAHO included a chapter on Information Management in its Accreditation Manual for Hospitals
   1. JCAHO felt that managing information resources is extremely important
   2. areas addressed
      a. identifying information needs
      b. design of the information management system
      c. definition and capture of data
      d. analysis and process of data into information
      e. reporting of data
      f. use of data
I. The accreditation manual
   1. emphasizes the requirements to document patient care
      a. assigns specific percentages of patient records that must comply with a given standard (i.e. an initial patient assessment must be found 100% of the time, whereas other required documentation ranges from 91-100%)
   2. describes requirements for medical record documentation as well as system-wide information requirements
   3. clinical service chapters provide information on specific record content
J. JCAHO uses a scoring guideline to determine compliance with the published standards

THE STANDARDS

I. 1994 JCAHO Standard Changes
   A. Ten (10) new Management of Information Standards (IM)
      1. facilities must take a hospital-wide approach to data capture, analysis and dissemination
      2. standards indicate concern for managing information for decision-making and not just data processing
      3. Expressing the 10 standards as questions can be helpful for self-evaluation
         a. How can data be evaluated?
         b. How can information be used?
         c. Are the people who need the data getting it?
         d. Is there a smooth flow of information?
   B. JCAHO publishes the Comprehensive Accreditation Manual for Hospitals
      1. states not only the standards but next to each standard is the "intent statement" (the intent statements define the standards and give examples and suggestions on better ways to comply with the JCAHO regulations)
      2. includes examples on how the standards may be implemented
   C. The 10 IM standards
      1. each IM standard had several "children" standards (i.e. IM.7 had 24 "satellite" standards in addition to the main one, the "parent" standard)
         a. the "children" standards were generally more specific
      2. many of the old medical record standards still exist; many have been moved to other standard categories, into the intent statements, or into the scoring guidelines

II. JCAHO 2003 Parent Standards

A. IM.1 The organization plans and designs information management processes to meet internal and external information needs.

B. IM.2 Confidentiality, security and integrity of data and information are maintained.

C. IM.3 Uniform data definitions and data capture methods are used whenever possible.

D. IM.4 The necessary expertise and tools are available for the analysis and transformation of data into information.

E. IM.5 Transmission of data and information is timely and accurate.

F. IM.6 Adequate integration and interpretation capabilities are provided.

G. IM.7 The organization defines, captures, analyzes, transforms, transmits and reports patient-specific information related to patient care processes and outcomes.

H. IM.8 The organization collects and analyzes aggregate data to support patient care and service delivery and operations.

I. IM.9 Knowledge-based information systems, resources and services meet the organization's needs.

J. IM.10 Comparative performance data and information are defined, collected, analyzed, transmitted, reported and used.

III Example

A. IM.7 - The hospital defines, captures analyzes, transforms, transmits and reports patient-specific information related to patient care processes and outcomes (much of IM.7 relates to documentation requirements in the medical record).

1. What is the basis for JCAHO determining that portions of this standard have not been meet and rendering a facility a Type I recommendation?

2. JCAHO Type I Recommendations

    a. A Type I Recommendation will require a facility to resolve the problem (e.g. delinquent medical records), <u>prior</u> to receiving the accreditation status. Any of the following would give an institution a Type I Recommendation (this information would be found in the scoring guidelines)

        i. The number of delinquent records is greater than 50 percent of the average monthly discharges

        ii. The number of medical records delinquent due to the absence of medical history and physical examination exceeds 9 or 2 percent of the average monthly discharges, whichever is greater

        iii. The number of medical records delinquent due to the absence of an operative report exceeds 9 or 2 percent of the average monthly operative procedures, whichever is greater

    b. calculating medical record delinquency rate

        i. Add total delinquencies for 3 months in a quarter and divide that number by 3 to get an average for each quarter. Continue this process until all four quarterly averages are calculated. Total the four quarterly averages and divide by four. This gives the TOTAL AVERAGE. This is the figure that JCAHO will use to make the decision about the organization's delinquency rate.

3. Conditional Accreditation is given if the total medical record delinquencies is equal to or exceeds twice the average monthly discharges (AMD) rate.

Go to the JCAHO web page (JCAHO.org). In the "search" section type in "delinquency" and you will see a link for 2004 Decision Process and Decision Rules for Critical Access Hospitals

---

RANDOM UNANNOUNCED SURVEYS

Since 1993, JCAHO has performed random unannounced surveys (RUSs). There are fixed topics for random unannounced surveys (RUSs). Under JCAHO's RUS policy, five percent of organizations accredited under the ambulatory care, behavioral health, home care (including pharmacies), hospital and long term care accreditation programs will receive a RUS. An organization can be selected between nine and 30 months after its full survey and will not receive any prior notice that a surveyor is coming. The surveyor will include a review of both "variable" and "fixed" performance areas. (source: http://www.jcaho.org)

Beginning January 1, 2006, the JCAHO will conduct all regular surveys on an unannounced basis. Health information professionals will need to be very diligent in assuring that the organization's delinquent record rate remain continuously compliant with the standards.

References for JCAHO

Comprehensive Accreditation Manual for Hospital: The Official Handbook
    Joint Commission on Accreditation of Healthcare Organizations (JCAHO)
    Oakbrook Terrace, IL

Health Information Management of a Strategic Resource, 2nd Edition
    Abdelhak, et. al.
    W. B. Saunders, 2001

Health Information Management Technology
    Johns, Merida
    AHIMA, 2002

Health Information Management
    LaTour and Eichenwald
    AHIMA, 2003

Web site for JCAHO: **http://www.jcaho.org**

INFORMATION SYSTEMS

THE HARDWARE

I. History Of Computers
    A. The evolution of health care systems
        1. First Generation through Fifth Generation Computers

II. Computer Components
    A. Input and output devices
    B. Central processing unit (CPU)
        1. Primary Memory/Random Access Memory (RAM)
        2. Arithmetic-Logic Unit (ALU)
        3. Control Unit
        4. registries
        5. buffers
    C. Peripherals
        1. keyboard
        2. monitors
        3. mouse
        4. printers
            a. impact
            b. ink-jet
            c. laser imaging
            d. print chains
        5. scanners
    D. Secondary storage
        1. Magnetic hard drive
        2. Compact Disk-Read Only Memory (CD-ROM)
        3. Compact Disk-Recordable (CD-R)
        4. Compact Disk-Rewritable (CD-RW)
        5. Digital Video Disk or Digital Versatile Disk (DVD)
            a   DVD-ROM
            b. DVD-R
            c. DVD-RW

III. Types of Computers

THE SOFTWARE

I. Computer Software
   A. Application programs
      1. word processing
      2. spreadsheets
      3. data bases
      4. graphics
      5. GUI
      6. multimedia
      7. integrated
   B. Programming languages
   C. Stages of evaluating and selecting software
      1. software screening
      2. software selection
         a. don't pay for features that will never be used
         b. don't underestimate the cost of modifications and software interfaces
         c. don't underestimate the cost of installation and implementation
         d. avoid being one of the first users
      3. software communication and design
      4. external software
         a. lower costs
         b. less risks
         c. high quality
         d. less time
         e. fewer resources needed
      5. internal software
         a. usually meets the exact needs of the users
         b. more flexible
         c. greater control
      6. prototypes

Prototypes

A prototype develops a preliminary model of systems. It is usually a smaller or scaled-down version of the system that is to be developed. The prototype continues until the complete system is developed.

---

         a. meets users' needs better
         b. quicker development time
         c. fewer errors
         d. more opportunity for change
         e. total development costs can be higher
         f. may not use resources efficiently

SYSTEMS

A system is a group of related components serving a common purpose to include computers, procedures and personnel. An information system is a system that manages the data needed by an organization. Analysis identifies the requirements for a new information system for an organization. Design is the blueprints or plans for a new system using the requirements from the analysis. A system analyst is the person responsible for analysis and design.

I. Computer Systems
   A. Operating systems e.g. MS Windows or Linux
   B. Artificial Intelligence [(AI) Expert systems]
   C. Decision Support Systems (DSS)

II. Computer Networks
   A. Telecommunications
      1. Internet
         a. E-mail
         b. World Wide Web (WWB)
         c. Browsers
         d. Encryption
         e. Personal Digital Assistants (PDAs)
      2. Intranet
      3. Extranet
      4. Internet Service Providers
      5. Applications Service Providers
      6. Transmission Media
         a. Electrical Cables
         b. Fiber optics
         c. Radio, Micro, Infrared Waves
   B. Local area networks (LANs)/wide area networks (WANs)
      1. electronic data interchange (EDI)
      2. use of networks in healthcare
   C. Star networks
   D. Ring networks
   E. Community Health Information Network Systems (CHINS)
   F. Standards/protocols
      1. Health-Level 7 (HL7)
      2. TCP/IP

III. INFORMATION SYSTEMS PLANNING
A. Steps
   1. develop overall objectives
   2. identify systems projects
   3. set priorities and select projects
   4. analyze resource requirements
   5. set schedules and determine deadlines
   6. develop the planning document
B. Strategic plans
   1. developed from the organization's strategic plan
C. Tactical plans
   1. developed for middle level managers
   2. developed from the strategic plans
D. Operational plans
   1. describe the detail resources needed to accomplish an activity
   2. developed from tactical plans

IV. Systems Development Life Cycle (SDLC)

> These are phases of developing an information system from the beginning to removing it for a new system. There are anywhere between five and seven stages, depending on how the stages are combined.

A. Problem recognition
   1. Reasons for initiating a system
      a. problem with existing system
      b. desire to investigate new opportunities
      c. increasing competition
      d. need to be more effective with data
      e. change in internal or external environment
B. Feasibility Study
   1. short term, less than one month
   2. assess the extent
   3. examine current system (hardware and software)
   4. determine costs
   5. evaluate benefits
   6. cost-benefit analysis

Feasibility Report

The feasibility report summarizes the results of the study and makes recommendations for a system for development. The report is reviewed by the appropriate managers/administrators and a decision is made.

C. Analysis
   1. study current system
   2. determine requirements for new system
   3. order components for system
   4. interview users
   5. documents/aids
      a. data dictionary
      b. data flow diagrams
      c. process specifications
      d. data models
      e. prototypes
      f. systems flowcharts

Systems Analysis Report

The analysis report summarizes the strengths and weaknesses of the existing system and the requirements for the new system. Included is information regarding those areas of the existing system that could be improved to meet user requirements.

D. Design
   1. select hardware
   2. select software
   3. functional diagrams to hierarchical diagrams
   4. input and output formats
   5. security
   6. staff requirements
   7. procedures and work flow
   8. design database
   9. review by users, managers etc.
   10. documents/aids
      a. data dictionary
      b. data flow diagrams
      c. process specifications
      d. data models
      e. prototypes
      f. systems flowcharts
      g. structure charts
      h. input/output design forms
   11. design constraints
      a. hardware
      b. cost
      c. schedule
      d. procedural and operating
      e. software and database

Systems Design Report

The design report summarizes the decisions made for the system design and prepares the way for systems implementation. The report includes hardware, software, personnel, communications, data base, procedures, training and maintenance design.

E. Systems acquisition

Vendor

An information systems vendor is a company that offers hardware, software, telecommunications systems, databases, information systems, personnel and other related resources to interested parties.

---

1. vendors
    a. general computer manufacturers
    b. computer dealers and distributors
    c. leasing companies
    d. software companies
    e. other related companies
2. construction
    a. preparation of the site
    b. installation of the equipment
    c. modification of programs if needed
    d. test procedures
    e. user's verification system
    f. write documentation
    g. training
3. conversion
    a. plan
    b. install software
    c. convert data
    d. begin operation
4. maintenance
    a. determine problem and make required changes
    b. evaluate impact of change
    c. modify program
    d. test modifications
    e. use modified system
F. System completion
    1. evaluation

V. Data Base Management Systems

Database
A structure that allows for the storage of data about multiple entities and the relationships among these entities. A database is useless unless the data can be used by application programs and updated and queried by the user.

A. The database hierarchy
B. Database models
    1. Relational model
    2. network model
    3. hierarchical model
    4. object-oriented models
C. Database administration
    1. data administrator
        a. responsible for the administrative functions associated with database and database management
        b. evaluates and selects the database management system
        c. manages the RFP from vendors
D. Database management concepts
    1. field
    2. record
    3. file
        a. data redundancy
            i.   data integrity
            ii. difficult data retrieval
E. Database management software
    1. update and storage of data
    2. catalog of descriptions of the data
    3. natural user interface
    4. transaction support
    5. utilities to ensure data integrity
    6. concurrent processing controls
    7. recovery services
    8. authorization controls

VI. COMPUTER TECHNOLOGIES
A. Optical disc technology
B. Scanning devices
C. Voice recognition

VII. INFORMATION SYSTEMS TOOLS
A. Flowcharts
B. Process flowcharts
C. Systems flowcharts
D. Procedure analysis flowcharts
E. Gantt charts
F. PERT Network

GLOSSARY OF COMPUTER RELATED TERMS

1. Application program
2. Analog computer
3. Address
4. Archive
5. Backup
6. Bus
7. Buffer
8. Bit
9. CPU
10. Clone
11. Communications Port
12. Computer System
13. Computer programs
14. Default drive
15. Disc drivers
16. Database
17. Density
18. Digital
19. Disk Operating System (DOS)
20. Disc drives
21. E-mail
22. Field
23. End-user
24. File query
25. File allocation Table
26. Floppy disc
27. Fourth-generation languages
28. Format
29. Gigabyte
30. Generational backup
31. Half-duplex
32. Hard drive
33. Hard copy
34. Hardware
35. kilobyte
36. I/O (in-put-output)
37. Laser printer
38. Mainframe
39. Memory
40. Megabyte
41. Microcomputer
42. Minicomputer
43. Modem
44. Multiple access unit
45. Network
46. Non-contiguous storage
47. Off-line
48. On-line
49. Operating system
50. Optical disc
51. Proprietary software
52. Pixel
53. Platter
54. Protocol
55. Parity bit
56. Query language
57. RAM
58. Real-time
59. ROM
60. Relational data model
61. Report generator
62. Signal
63. Softcopy
64. Software
65. Spreadsheet
66. Synchronous transmission
67. Tape
68. Telecommunications
69. Word-processing
70. Write Once Read Many (WORM)

References for Information Systems

Books:

Health Information Management, A Strategic Resource, 2nd Edition
  Abdelhak, M., Grostick, S., Hanken, M. A., and Jacobs, E. (2001)
  W. B. Saunders. *Philadelphia*, PA

Health Information Management Technology: An applied approach
  Johns, M. L. (2002)
  American Health Information Management Association. Chicago, IL

Information Management for Health Professions, 2nd Edition
  Johns, M. L., (2002)
  Delmar Publishers. Albany, NY

Health Information Management: Concepts Principles and Practice
  LaTour, K.M. and Eichenwald, S. (2002)
  American Health Information Management Association. Chicago, IL

Health Management Information Systems, Methods and Practical Applications, 2nd Edition
  Tan, J. K. (2001)
  Aspen Publishers Inc. Gaithersburg, MD

AHIMA Articles:

"To "E" or not to "E": HIM and the dawn of e-health".
  Fuller, S. (2000)
  Journal of AHIMA, 71(4), 50-53.

"Implementing an electronic imaging system".
  Graham, D. (2000)
  Journal of AHIMA, 71(2), 20-23.

"Document imaging and workflow technology in healthcare today".
  Mahoney, M. E. (1997)
  Journal of AHIMA, 68(4), 28-36.

"The use of XML in healthcare information management".
  Seals, M. (2000)
  Journal of Healthcare Information Management, 14(2), 85-95.

"XML: Defining the transition from paper to digital record".
  Peters, Jr., R. M. (2000)
  Journal of AHIMA, 71(1), 34-38.

"Do you need an ASP ASAP?"
  Sheridan, C. (2001)
  Journal of AHIMA, 72(8), 38-42.

"Documentation goes wireless: A look at mobile healthcare computing devices".
  Waegemann, C.P., and Tessier, C. (2002)
  Journal of AHIMA, 73(8), 36-39.

MANAGEMENT

THE FUNCTIONS: PLANNING

I. Planning
    A. Characteristics
    B. Participants
    C. Planning Process
    D. Strategic Plans
    E. Long term vs. short term planning
    F. Product Line/Service Line Management
        1. focus is on process and meeting the needs of the "customer"
        2. HIM product lines
            a. record completion services
            b. data and information services
            c. record maintenance services
            d. transcription services

II. Strategic Planning/Management

> *the art and science of formulating, implementing and evaluating cross-functional decisions in order to achieve the objectives*

    A. Strategic Skills
    B. Elements of Strategic Management
        1. vision
        2. issues
        3. goals
        4. strategies
        5. tactics

III. Types Of Plans
    A. Philosophy Statements
        1. Mission statements
    B. Goals/Objectives
        1. developed from mission statements
    C. Policies
        1. Facility
        2. Department
        3. Developing policies
            a. sources of information
            b. new or revised
            c. format
    D. Procedures
        1. writing procedures
            a. sources of information
            b. new or revised
            c. format
    E. Methods
    F. Rules
    G. Policy and Procedure Manuals

IV. Planning Tools
   A. MBO
   B. Interviewing
   C. Questionnaires

V. Time Management
   A. Prioritize
      1. urgent
      2. important/not urgent
      3. unimportant
   B. Delegate
      1. delegate authority with responsibility

VI. Decision Making/Problem Solving
   A. Problem Solving
      1. Problem Identification
      2. Approach to Problem Solving
         a. routine
         b. scientific
         c. creative
         d. quantitative
      3. Group Problem Solving
         a. Quality Circles
   B. Decision Making
      1. The Process
      2. The Steps
      3. Bases for the Decision
         a. influences
         b. constraints
   C. Decision Making Tools
      1. Decision tables
      2. Decision grid/decision matrix
      3. Decision Tree
   D. Group Decision Making Techniques
      1. consensus building
      2. brainstorming
      3. nominal group techniques
      4. intuition and satisficing
      5. Delphi technique
      6. bounded rationality
   E. Programmed and Non-programmed Decisions

THE FUNCTIONS: ORGANIZING

I. Introduction to Organizing
    A. Process
    B. Concepts and Principles
    C. Formal vs. Informal Organization

II. Authority and Responsibility
    A. Types of authority
        1. Line
        2. Staff
        3. Function
        4. Lines of Authority
            a. Unity of Command
            b. Span of Control
            c. Departmentalization
    B. Managerial Power
        1. coercive power
        2. reward power
        3. legitimate power
        4. expert power

III. Organizational Structure
    A. Centralization vs. Decentralization
    B. Matrix
    C. Informal vs. Formal organization
    D. Departmentalization

IV. Delegation
    A. Barriers
        1. manager's attitude (they feel that delegating is a waste of time)
        2. manager's inability to say "no" (managers should resist the idea to take over when employees ask for help)
        3. not training employees well
        4. not scheduling meetings to help employees stay on track
    B. Common Mistakes
        1. vague instructions
        2. not enough training given to the delegatee
        3. not giving the employee the authority that is needed to fulfill the responsibility
    C. Delegation Musts
        1. define what and how you want to delegate
        2. be sure that both parties understand the terms of the delegated task
        3. train and orient the delegatee well
        4. offer feedback to the delegatee
        5. increase responsibilities as the delegatee demonstrates ability and skill

V. Tools Of Organizational Analysis And Staffing
A. Organizing People
1. Organizational Charts
   a. purpose
   b. types
   c. advantages/disadvantages
2. Job Analysis
   a. definition
   b. purpose
   c. collection of data
3. Job description
   a. definition
   b. uses/purposes
   c. cements
   d. guidelines for writing
B. Organizing the Work
1. Work Distribution Charts
2. Work scheduling
3. Procedures
4. Procedure flow charts
5. Methods of work division
   a. serial work division
   b. parallel work division
   c. unit work division
C. Job Design
1. position enrichment
2. position enlargement
3. position rotation
4. job sharing
5. compressed workweek

VI. Committees As An Organizational Tool
A. Nature of Committees
B. Functions of Committees
C. Composition of the Committee
D. Advantages of Committees and Meetings
E. Committee Meetings
1. creating an effective meeting
2. participates
   a. chairperson
   b. members
3. agenda items
4. chairing the meeting
5. rules regarding formality of meetings
F. Documentation of Meetings
1. agenda
2. minutes
   a. formats
3. action that is to take place

THE FUNCTIONS: DIRECTING

I. **Directing/Actuating**
   A. Theories of motivation
      1. Maslow
      2. Herzberg
      3. McGregor
   B. Management Skills
      1. conceptual skills
      2. interpersonal skills
      3. self-monitoring
      4. technical
   C. Conflict management
      1. Personal
      2. Small Group
      3. Organizational
      4. Strategies
   D. Leadership
      1. styles
      2. concepts
      3. sources of
   E. Mentoring
   F. Motivating
      1. incentives
      2. job enlargement
      3. job enrichment
      4. job sharing
   G. Work simplification
      1. "work smarter not harder" (i.e. determine how to accomplish a task with less effort in less time)
      2. Tools
         a. flow process chart
         b. work flow chart
         c. flow chart
         d. movement diagram
   H. Project Management
      1. uses the basic management principles to complete a project successfully
      2. project management techniques
      3. project management tools
         a. Gantt Chart
         b. PERT Network
   I. Continuous Quality Improvement (CQI)
      1. assessing and improving existing systems
      2. improvement models
         a. FOCUS-PDCA
         b. Lanley, Nolan, and Nolan Foundation For Improvement/PDSA

3. CQI Techniques and Tools
    a. brainstorming
    b. affinity grouping
    c. nominal group technique
    d. multivoting technique
    e. root cause analysis/fishbone diagram
    f. Pareto chart
    g. force-field analysis
    h. check sheet
J. Re-engineering
    1. purpose
        a. reduce cost
        b. increase revenue
        c. improve quality
        d. reduce risk
K. Change Management
    1. change agent
    2. promote change
        a. survey feedback
        b. team building
        c. appreciative inquiry
    3. stages of change
    4. resistance to change
    5. facilitating change
    6. reflection

II. Communication
A. Process of communicating
    1. barriers
        a. time constraints
        b. language
        c. emotions
        d. non-verbal cues
    2. overcoming barriers
        a. feedback skills
        b. empathy skills
        c. listening skills
        d. language simplification
    3. components
    4. techniques
    5. oral and written
    6. informal communication
        a. grapevine
B. Methods of disseminating information
    1. letters
    2. memos
    3. reports
    4. meeting minutes

THE FUNCTIONS: CONTROLLING

(See also Financial Management Outline)

I. Controlling
   A. The Control Process
   B. Characteristics of Adequate Controls

II. Establishing Standards
   A. Definition
   B. Types of Standards
   C. Methods of Establishing Standards
     1. Past Experience
     2. Appraisal
     3. Scientific Method
       a. stopwatch studies
       b. work sampling
     4. Published Standards

III. Productivity
   A. Productivity monitors
     1. Work measurement for standards and staffing
       a. standard time data
       b. past performance record
       c. simulation
     2. Work Measurement for Quantity Control
       a. employee reported logs
       b. stop watch time studies
       c. work sampling
     3. Work Measurement for Quality Control
       a. checklist
       b. audit
       c. inspection
       d. questionnaire
       e. report

IV. Controlling Charts/Tools
   A. Gantt chart
   B. PERT network
   C. flow chart
   D. questionnaires
   E. surveys

VI. Work Simplification Tools
   A. Flow Process Chart
   B. Work Flow Chart
   C. Application of Technique

ERGONOMICS

I. Office Space And Environment Planning
   A. Ergonomic Principles
      1. noise control
      2. high technology equipment
      3. lighting
      4. heating, ventilation and air conditioning
      5. esthetics
      6. furniture
   B. Departmental Locations and Space Requirements
      1. departmental functions and activities
      2. functional interdepartmental relationships
      3. accessibility to medical staff
      4. work flow patterns
      5. structural factors
         a. electrical
         b. weight
         c. lighting
         d. cooling/heating/ventilation
   C. Office Space Planning
      1. analysis process
      2. blue print study
      3. layout preparation and workflow
      4. other considerations
      5. planning the office move
         a. movement diagram
   D. Equipment Planning
      1. selection
      2. maintenance
      3. depreciation
   E. Office Furniture
      1. office chairs
      2. office desks
      3. modular furniture
      4. cabinets and stands
      5. other
   F. Office Environment
      1. lighting
      2. color
      3. music and Sound
      4. climate
      5. personnel preferences
   G. Design the Work Space
      1. work Flow
      2. traffic patterns
      3. sharing workspace
      4. personnel needs of employees
      5. tools
         a. movement diagram
         b. trip frequency chart
         c. proximity chart

PROJECT MANAGEMENT

I. Managing Projects
   A. Focus on cost, schedule and quality
   B. Project management life cycle
      1. project definition
      2. planning and organizing
      3. tracking and analysis
      4. project revisions
      5. change control
      6. communication
   C. Project Manager
      1. skills of project manager
         a. general management skills
         b. leadership skills
         c. communication skills
         d. facilitation skills
         e. analytical skills
      2. functions of project manager
         a. define the project expectations
         b. create the project plan and gather the project team
         c. manage the project
         d. recommend revisions
         e. execute change
         f. communicate project information (orally and written)
   D. Project team
      1. types of team structure
         a. functional
         b. by project
         c. matrix

References for Management

Health Information: Management of a Strategic Resource 2nd Edition
   Abdelhak, Mervat, Grostick, Sara, Hanken, Mary Alice, and Jacobs, Ellen
   W. B. Saunders Company. Philadelphia, PA

Health Information Management An Applied Approach
   Johns, Merida, et. al. (2002)
   American Health Information Management Association (AHIMA). Chicago IL

Health Information Management Concepts, Principles and Practice
   LaTour and Eichenwald (2002)
   American Health Information Management Association (AHIMA). Chicago IL

Management Principles for Health Professionals
   Liebler, Joan Gratto, and McConnell, Charles, R. (1999)
   Jones and Bartlett Publishers (acquired from Aspen Publishing). Sudbury, MA

Management of Health Information
   Mattingly, Rozella (1997)
   Delmar Publishing. Albany, NY

HUMAN RESOURCE MANAGEMENT

I. Human Resource Management
   A. Planning and Analysis
   B. Staffing
   C. HR Development
   D. Compensation and Benefits
   E. Employee and Labor Management Relations
   F. Equal Employment Opportunity

II. Role of the HIM Manager in Human Resources
   A. All levels of management (supervisory, middle and top) are responsible for human resources.
   B. Tools for HR planning
      1. job descriptions
      2. work schedules
      3. performance standards
      4. policy and procedure manuals

STAFFING

I. Development Of The Job Position
   A. Job analysis
      1. elements
      2. components
         a. tasks involved
         b. skills or qualifications
         c. job environment
         d. job pressures
   B. Job specifications (describe the requirements)
      1. elements
         a. skills
         b. education
         c. previous experience
      2. components
   C. Job description
      1. elements
         a. developed from analysis and specifications
         b. describes tasks involved
         c. states conditions under which holder of job will work
      2. components
   D. Recruitment
      1. internal
      2. external
   E. Screening
      1. Interviewing
         a. get a "feel" of candidate
         b. clarify qualifications
   F. Selection
   G. Hiring
   H. Retention of staff

HUMAN RESOURCE DEVELOPMENT

I. Initial Training
    A. Orientation
1. gives new employees an idea of organization's goals and values, policies and procedures
2. policies (overtime, payday, termination procedures, employee conduct, dress codes)
3. benefit programs (insurance, vacation)
4. job duties and responsibilities

    B. Consultations
    C. Professional organizations
    D. Vendors
    E. In-service
    F. On-the-job
    G. Supervisory
    H. Correspondence courses

II. Ongoing Training and Development of Personnel
    A. Defining of training need
    B. Setting of objectives (behavioral in nature)
    C. Selecting training methods
    D. Selecting and scheduling employees to be trained
    E. Doing the training
    F. Follow-up and evaluation training

III. Tools for Human Resource Planning
    A. Replacement Charts
    B. Staffing Tables
    C. Human Resource Audits
    D. Skill Inventories

IV. Performance Appraisal
    A. Objectives
    B. Use job description
    C. Dos and Don'ts
    D. Measuring performance against standard
1. collect data on employee performance
2. evaluate employee performance

V. Disciplinary Action

A. Progressive
   1. warning
      a. oral
      b. written
   2. suspension
   3. termination

B. Documentation   (*If you didn't document it, it didn't happen*)
   1. Date(s) of incident(s)
   2. Who was involved in the incident? Who was present at the conference?
   3. What happened (only the facts)?
   4. Why was the incident considered to be improper?
   5. What did the employee say he/she was going to do?
   6. What will happen if there are any more occurrences?
   7. Date and time for follow-up
   8. Management's desire to see the employee succeed; faith in the employee's ability to succeed
   9. signatures

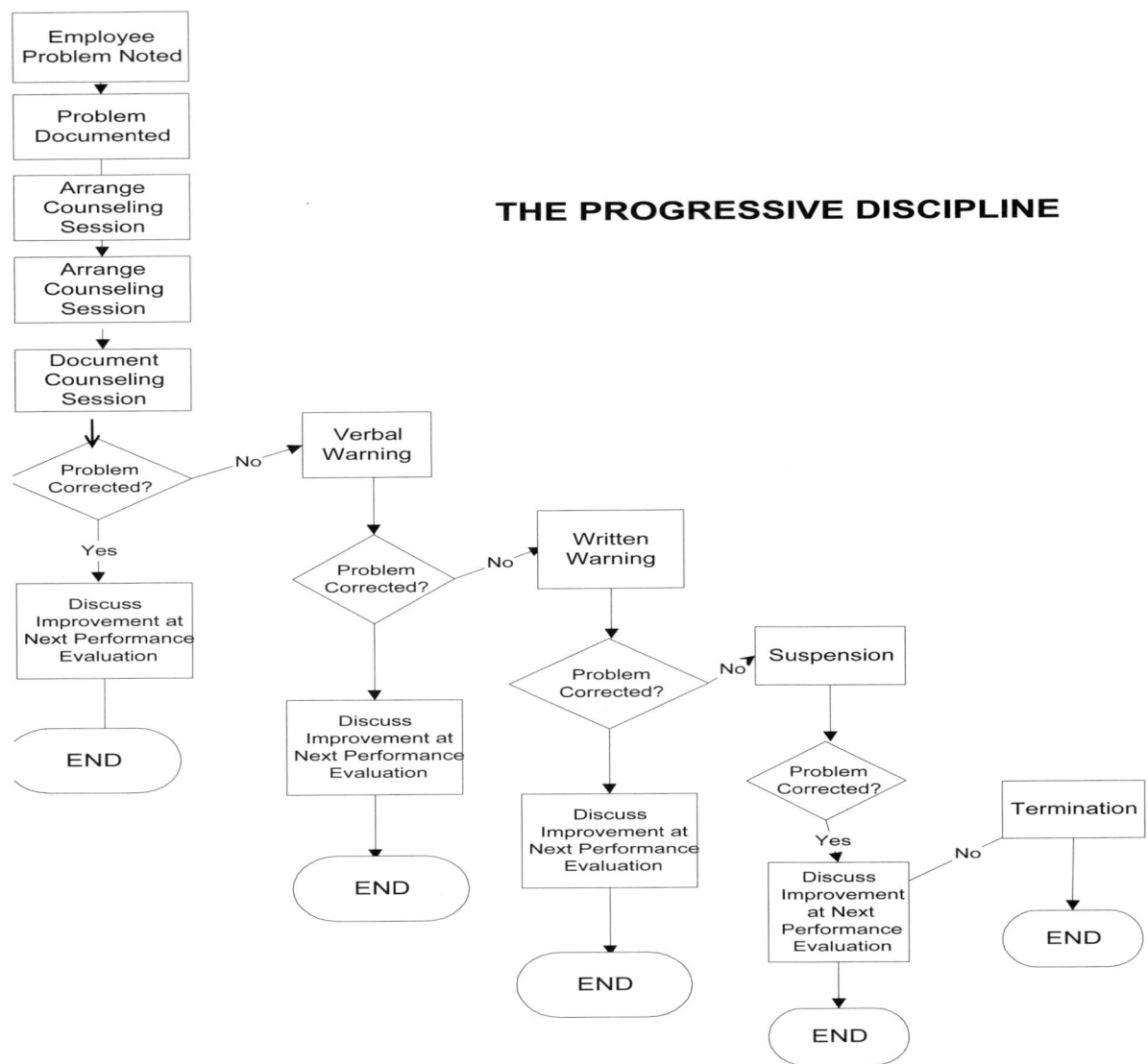

THE PROGRESSIVE DISCIPLINE

COMPENSATION AND BENEFITS

I. Wage and Salary Administration

> **Compensation**
> *Compensation is a combination of payments, benefits and employer services. It is a factor in motivating employees.*

A. Wages and salaries
1. wages based on calculation of the number of hours worked or the number of units produced. Wages provide a direct incentive to workers.
2. salaries base compensation on units of a week, month or year. Salaried workers such as managers and professionals normally receive no overtime pay, but have more flexibility in their working time.

B. Benefits and service

> **Employee Benefits**
> *Fringe benefits are financial benefits other than wages, salaries, and incentives which organizations provide to their employees. Administrators or executives sometimes receive additional benefits known as "perks". Organizations provide health and safety programs for all workers although it is hard to estimate their value in dollars.*

1. insurance plans
   a. social security (mandatory)
      i. purpose is to provide funds for employee at retirement
   b. unemployment benefits (mandatory)
      i. if employee is laid off or quits, employers pay into a fund
      ii. if unrelated to performance, employee is entitled to collect benefits
   c. death (life insurance)
   d. health and dental insurance plans
   e. disability insurance
   f. retirement benefits, exclusive of social security (Pension Plans)
2. holiday pay
3. sick pay
4. vacation pay
5. overtime pay

C. Job evaluations
1. rating
2. job classification
3. point method
4. factor comparison method

D. Merit Increases

E. Incentive Programs

> **Incentive Programs**
>
> *Incentives are rewards linked to a certain level of productivity or profitability for individuals such as managers, directors, administrators etc. They are given in the form of bonuses, commissions, profit sharing or production sharing.*

1. A bonus is a payment in addition to a regular salary or wage, usually given annually.
2. Commissions are payments based on sales made.
3. Profit sharing is a system in which employees receive a portion of the organization's profits.
4. Production sharing is a plan similar to profit sharing, but the rewards are ties to cost savings from increased profits. This is designed for production workers rather than managers since it is believed that workers have a greater impact on production (transcriptionists are an example).

EMPLOYEE AND LABOR/MANAGEMENT RELATIONS AND LAWS

I. **Labor Relations**
  A. Union's and management's rights
    1. functions of unions
      a. promote the general welfare of its members
      b. marketing the unions (selling the union itself)
      c. get better wages for members
      d. negotiate and administer labor agreements for members
      e. protect members from arbitrary management actions
      f. enhance the position of the employees with management
      g. provide a socializing mechanism for membership
      h. focus on wages, benefits and job security
    2. organizing union - guidelines
      a. thirty percent of employees must demonstrate an interest
      b. petition NLRB to monitor vote
      c. if election is won by unions, it has one year to negotiate for a collective bargaining contract
      d. if no contract is agreed upon after a year, the whole process starts again
    3. management's cans and cannots during union organizing
    4. bargaining unit
    5. closed and open shop
    6. grievance
    7. violations
    8. unions and human rights management
    9. exclusions
  B. Five types of bargaining units in hospitals
    1. RN's
    2. other professional employees
    3. LPNs and technical employees
    4. clerical employees
    5. service and maintenance employees
  C. During a union organizing campaign the manger should not
    1. threaten employees about what may happen if they join the union
    2. promise them any reward for staying out of the union
    3. interrogate employees about their preferences for or against the union
    4. question union members about union matters or meetings
    5. have private discussion with employee about union activities
    6. ask employees how they will vote
    7. hold a meeting with an employee within 24 hours of the election
  D. During a union organizing campaign the manger should not
    1. threaten employees about what may happen if they join the union
    2. promise them any reward for staying out of the union
    3. interrogate employees about their preferences for or against the union
    4. question union members about union matters or meetings
    5. have private discussion with employee about union activities
    6. ask employees how they will vote
    7. hold a meeting with an employee within 24 hours of the election

E. Common union terminology
    1. bargaining unit
    2. collective bargaining
    3. negotiations
    4. mediation
    5. arbitration
F. Unfair union labor practices
    1. coercion of employees
    2. discrimination
    3. not bargaining in good faith (good faith means an honest attempt to reach an agreement)
G. Impact of union on the employee
    1. cost of union membership
    2. forced through assessments to support striking workers of other companies and unions
    3. Equalizes the employee by virtue of the union contract. Every union employee is the same therefore equating the worst employee with the best. Only the length of the service is important (not ability or merit).
    4. Bargaining begins at zero. Bargaining does not begin with what you already have (employees can end up with less than they already have in terms of wages and benefits).
    5. The only real weapon the employee has is to strike. When that happens, the employee loses wages that are never recovered.
    6. You are not allowed to take your problem to management. You must go to your collective bargaining unit.
    7. Union officials do not always have the employee's best interest in mind.
H. Federal labor laws
    1. National Labor Relations Act/Wagner Act (NRLA)
        a. gave workers the right to organize and bargain collectively
    2. National Labor Relations Board (NLRB)
        a. oversees labor issues based on the labor laws
    4. Taft-Hartley Act
        a. placed restrictions on union activities
    5. Landrum-Griffin Act
        a. eliminated improper activities toward union members by unions and management
    6. American Disability Act
        a. What is a disability?
        b. employer compliance with
    7. Fair Labor Standard Act (FLSA)
        a. established a federal minimum wage with time and a half for overtime; equal pay for equal work; exempted hospitals until 1966
        b. exempt: salary employees
            i. exempt from labor laws regarding overtime
        c. non-exempt: hourly paid employees
            i. labor laws regarding overtime apply
    8. Civil Rights Act
        a. bans discrimination on the basis of race, color, religion, sex or national origin
    9. Equal Pay Act (amendment to the FLSA)
        a. prohibited wage differentials based upon sex
    10. Age Discrimination in Employment Act
        a. bans discrimination against employment of persons 40 to 70 years
    11. Equal Employment Opportunity Act
        a. strengthens the Civil Rights Act (provides for affirmative action programs)

References for Human Resources

Administrative Office Management 12th Edition
Odgers, Pattie and Kelling, B. Lewis
Published by: Thompson Learning (South-Western Educational Publishing)

The Effective Health Care Supervisor, 4th Edition
McConnell, Charles R.
Published by: Jones & Bartlett (previously by Aspen)

Health Information: Management of a Strategic Resource, 2nd Edition
Abdelhak, Mervat; Grostick, Sara; Hanken, Mary Alice; Jacobs, Ellen; editors
Published by: W. B. Saunders (Harcourt Health Sciences Company)

Health Information Management: Concepts, Principles, and Practice
LaTour, Kathleen L. and Eichenwald, Shirley; editors
Published by: the American Health Information Management Association (AHIMA)

Health Information Management Technology: An Applied Approach
Johns, Merida L., Editor
Published by: the American Health Information Management Association (AHIMA)

Introduction to Health Information Technology
Davis, Nadina and Lacour, Melissa
Published by W. B. Saunders (Harcourt Health Sciences Company) 2002

Management Principles for Health Professions 2nd Edition
Liebler, Joan Gratto; Levine, Ruth Ellen; Rothman, Jeffrey
Published by: Jones & Bartlett (previously by Aspen)

Management of Health Information Functions and Applications
Mattingly, Rozella
Published by: Delmar Learning

Management Skills for the New Health Care Supervisor, 3rd Edition
Umiker, William
Published by: Jones & Bartlett (previously by Aspen)

FINANCIAL MANAGEMENT

THE BASICS

I. Accounting Principles
A. Debits and credits
B. Assets are items or resources that belong to the organization and have a future value (i.e. furniture, copy machines, land).
C. Liabilities are amounts owed to various creditors and vendors (i.e. bills that the organization owes such as wages or mortgage payments).
D. Revenues and expenses (revenues are the moneys received for services provided; expenses are the costs to provide a service)
E. Equity is the difference between revenues and expenses.

II. Managerial Accounting

MANAGERIAL ACCOUNTING
Activities of planning and preparing budgets consistent with strategic plans

A. Report preparation
   1. Involves the current and future activities (budgets, productivity etc)
B. Cost accounting (identifying and isolating the cost of producing goods and services)
   1. chart of accounts
      a. standard developed by the AHA to assign designated accounts for a specific transaction
   2. responsibility centers
   3. cost centers

III. Financial Accounting
A. Records and reports the financial transactions of the organization
   1. past and current orders, payments, expenses, revenues etc.
   2. captures the data necessary to build the foundation for reports
   3. HIM more involved with this aspect of accounting

IV. Recording Financial Transactions
A. Debit and credit
B. Journal entries
   1. types of accounts (accounts payable, cash, inventory, etc.)

V. Financial Statements
   A. Balance Sheet
      1. indicates items owned or controlled by organization
      2. indicates debts owed by organization
      3. indicates ownership or interest in the organization
      4. by definition, the balance sheet must balance

Balance Sheet Equation

Assets + Liabilities = Owners Equity

   B. Income Statement
      1. summarizes the organization's operations at a particular point in time
      2. includes revenues that the organization generates
      3. shows the "bottom line"

VI. Analyzing Financial Statements
   A. Ratios are comparisons of one item to another to express the size of an item in relation to the other.

Example: What is the ratio of sunny days to rainy days

$$\frac{\textit{Number of sunny days}}{\textit{Number of rainy days}}$$

   B. Liquidity Ratios
      1. shows how liquid or cash-free the organization is
      2. ability to cover current debts out of cash reserves or other assets
      3. most common liquidity ratio is current ratio
         a. indicates the organization's ability to pay its current liabilities

---

Current Ratio

$$\frac{\textit{Current Assets}}{\textit{Current Liabilities}} \quad \frac{100{,}000}{50{,}000} = 2.0$$

Explanation:
For each $1 of current liability, there are $2 of current assets available to cover debt

---

      4. Acid-test ratio
         a. compares current liabilities to current liquid assets

---

Acid-Test Ratio

$$\frac{\text{Cash + short-term investments + net current receivables}}{\text{total current liabilities}} \quad \frac{650{,}000}{200{,}000} = 3.25$$

Explanation:
For every dollar of current liabilities there are 3.25 of current assets that could be sold quickly to offset liabilities if needed.

C. Activity Ratios (Turnover Ratios)
  1. help to determine how effective an organization is in utilizing its assets in the management of the organization

Activity Ratio
patient accounts receivable / average daily patient revenues
Explanation: Average time that receivables are outstanding

D. Performance Ratios
  1. evaluate the use of resources to achieve a goal; uses the operating margin ratio
     a. The operating margin ratio shows the relationship between the net revenues received and the expenses required to supply the revenues. It is a measure of profitability.

Operating Margin Ratio	
Operating gain / total operating revenue	$2,5000,000 = .0357 or 3.6% / $70,000,000
Explanation: There is a 3.6% profit after expenses	

E. Statement of cash flow
F Statement of retained earnings
G Statement of stockholder's equity

THE SPECIFICS

I. Budgets

BUDGETS
Numerical documents that translate the goals and objectives into forecasts of volume and monetary resources needed

A. Forecasting the Budget
  1. initial acquisition costs
     a. one time costs associated with purchasing equipment
     b. costs to include
        i.   purchase price
        ii. installation costs
        iii. remodeling costs
        iv. training and consulting costs
  2. operational costs
     a. includes the yearly costs to operate the equipment
        i.   rental and lease
        ii. maintenance agreements
        iii. direct labor
        iv. supplies and materials
        v.   space

3. operational and other benefits
   a. the savings gained from the acquisitions operational
B. Budget Process
   1. operations budgets
      a. predict the labor, supply and other expenses required to support the work volume predicted
         i. wages and salaries projected
         ii. expenses projected supplies (i.e. file folders, paper)
         iii. project any department revenues (i.e. correspondence)
   2. compare current and proposed budgets
C. Types or Methods of Budgets
   1. preparation
      a. budgets may be prepared for one year or several years
      b. typically budgets are prepared for 12 months
   2. rolling budget method
      a. budget is prepared for a period of time and at the end of that time another month is added
   3. flexible budget
      a. predicated on volume
      b. all labor and expenses are predicted based on anticipated volume
   4. zero-based budgets
      a. required to re-evaluate and justify department's needs annually
      b. a much more tedious and time consuming process
D. Master Budget
   1. all revenues and expenses for the total organization are consolidated
E. Cash Budget
   1. estimates of future cash receipts and disbursements
   2. predicts when cash will be received and disbursed
F. Budget Cycle
   1. fiscal period
      a. budgets correspond to fiscal periods
      b. the organization can choose the fiscal period to be
         a. calendar year
         b. or any time of the year
      c. fiscal periods are selected by organization based on what is best for them (organizations may have different fiscal periods)
   2. interim period
      a. any time frame less than the entire fiscal year
      b. indicates variances in budget

II. Operating Budgets
   A. Expense budget
   B. Revenue budget

> The revenue and expense budget estimates the gross revenues (incoming money) and gross expenditures (outgoing money.)

   C. Personnel/staffing budget
   D. Purpose
   1. budgets must account for
      a. staffing projections
      b. external influences
      c. fixed and variable costs
      d. direct and indirect expenses
   E. Revenue and Expense Budget
   1. Most common type of budget (When you refer to your budget you are really speaking of the R&E.)

> Revenue reflects anticipated revenues (i.e. sales, payment of services, grants, endowments). The largest source is patient services. HIA revenues is a very small portion of HID's overall budget. In many circumstances, since revenue is such a small amount, it is completed, but not given a great deal of consideration.
>
> Expenses are the costs of operating the facility such as supplies, purchased services, salaries and wages, employee benefits, etc.

   2. Expenses are divided into various categories (Uniform Code of Accounts)
      a. depreciation
      b. insurance
      c. books
      d. memberships
      e. salaries, benefits, supplies etc.
   3. Wages and benefits (greatest expense)
      a. more than fifty percent of a facility's total expense is due to wages, salaries and benefits
      b. personnel budgets are projections based on number of personnel hours needed and the costs associated with vacation, relief and overtime pay, temporary and/or seasonal help
   4. Direct vs. Indirect Expenses
      a. direct
         i. salaries
         ii. services and contracts
         iii. dues and subscriptions
         iv. equipment
      b. indirect
         i. charged to department on a formula basis or some process of assessment
         ii. may include equipment depreciation, telephone costs, maintenance and repairs, physical plant operations and building depreciation

F. Variances
   1. Variances are the differences between the revenues and expenses, or what actually occurred vs. what was predicted or "budgeted" to occur.
   2. The planned expenditures are compared to the actual expenditures (budget variance reports).
   3. Corrective action is taken if deviation is significant (i.e. are revenues in excess of expenses).
   4. Throughout the year (monthly and/or quarterly) a manager receives a periodic report indicating how much has been spent up to that date vs. what was budgeted for the same time period. It identifies for the manager whether he/she is operating the department within the acceptable levels of the budget.
G. Variance reports
   1. Manager reviews the regular reports, looking for any differences
   2. Manager must justify (give an explanation) for any variances from the budget
   3. A variance may be unfavorable, over budget
   4. A variance may be favorable, under budget
   5. Variances may or may not represent a problem
   6. A department may be under or over budget and still be within acceptable parameters
   7. Some variance is always expected

The formula for calculating a budget variance:

actual - budget = variance

If supplies were budgeted at $5000 and the amount that was actually spent was $3,500, the budget variance would be $1,500. Since this is under the budgeted amount, it is considered to be favorable (favorable amounts may still require an explanation). When the variance is over the budgeted amount, it is considered to be unfavorable.

Frequently the variance is viewed as a percentage rather than a whole number.

$$\frac{\text{actual - budget}}{\text{budget}} \times 100 = \text{variance percentage}$$

H. Personnel budget (staffing) and justification
   1. To control personnel costs you must control the positions. Determine
      a. what positions are needed
      b. when they should be filled
      c. what salary is appropriate for the positions
I. Factors considered with budget calculations
   1. Personnel costs are calculated in terms of budgeted positions
   2. Budget for each position (i.e. clerical, technician, supervisors)
   3. pay rates for each number of FTEs
   4. total personnel cost is most frequently based on workload (number of discharges)

III. Purchasing
    A. Purchase Orders
        1. requires authorization
        2. sent to accounts payable
    B. Shipping and Receiving Documents
        1. description of items purchased
    C. Invoices
        1. request for payment
    D. Statements
        1. list of outstanding invoices
    E. Inventory Slips
        1. tracking of purchased items

IV. Capital Budgets

Capital Budgets

Planning for capital equipment acquisition and renovations is part of the annual budgeting process. It involves integrating long and short term operating needs as it relates to equipment. Capital equipment has an acquisition cost in excess of a stated amount (usually $300-$500), a useful life of more than one year and is large enough to be identified with a tag of some kind. The cost of the equipment is not charged to an expense account. It is carried on the balance sheet and depreciated over the course of its useful life.

    A. Reasons for Capital Requests
        1. requests are typically originated by department director
        2. requests are for/to
            a. replacement
            b. improve productivity
            c. improve quality of service
            d. meet accreditation requirements
            e. new service
            f. other (i.e. expand a service, improve safety conditions, increase equipment capacity, reduce costs or improve patient care or convenience)
    B. Capital Expenditure Committee
        1. evaluates capital requests to ensure that the requests responded to will be the most beneficial to the organization
    C. Money and Time
        1. an investment decision is based on time and money
            a. length of time the money is invested
            b. degree of risk associated with the investment
            c. Is it more beneficial to receive a dollar today or a dollar one year from now?

D. Assessment of an investment
    1. use capital evaluation methods
        a. net present value
        b. return on investment (ROI)
        c. payback method
        d. accounting rate of return
    2. net present value (NPV)
        a. when comparing two alternatives, the one with the higher NPV should be selected

---

NPV

NPV is the difference between the present value of cash inflows and the present value of the investment. The present value of cash inflows is attained by discounting the cash inflows from a project at a rate equal to the organization's "cost of capital". In other words, this expresses the value of funds received in the future in current terms.

$10 received 3 years from now is not the same as $10 received today.
It undoubtedly will have a lower value.

NPV= discounted cash inflows less discounted cash outflows

---

    3. pay back method

Pay Back Period

The payback period is the amount of time it takes for the annual cash flow to "repay" the investment. In other words, it determines the number of years it will take for the cash inflows from each project to payback the initial investment, or cash outflows.

$$\frac{\text{Net investment}}{\text{annual cash flow}} = \text{payback period} \qquad \frac{\$120{,}000}{\$30{,}000} = 4 \text{ years}$$

---

    4. rate of return

Average Rate of Return

This method uses averages. The annual net inflows or outflows are averages over the project's life. The investment value is also averaged over the life of the project.

$$\frac{\text{Average profit}}{\text{Average investment}} = \text{average rate of return} \qquad \frac{\$15{,}000}{\$60{,}000} = .25 \text{ or } 25\%$$

V. Productivity

> *Productivity can be defined as the number of items produced per staff hour that meet established levels of quality and quantity.*
>
> Productivity is often expressed as a ratio of: $\frac{Output}{Input}$

A. Identifying standards

> *A standard is a statement of expected results, behavior or attitude. A performance standard states how well the work should be done and it also provides a means for the performance payment system.*

B. Set Productivity Standards
   1. measure the input
   2. measure the output
C. Develop productivity and control measures and monitors
D. Use standards
   1. for budget planning
   2. to determine staffing levels
   3. to develop work schedules
E. Justifying new positions based on productivity levels
F. Performance/productivity variances
G. Monitoring performance to determine staffing levels, turnaround time, productivity levels, workflow etc.
   1. develop/create tools to monitor productivity
H. Work sampling
   1. method of collecting performance data
   2. methodology
      a. population
      b. sample
      c. random selection
I. Benchmarking
   1. method of setting standards
   2. compares one organization's performance with one that has a reputation for excellence

VI. Financial Reports

A. Requests For Proposals (RFP)

> **RFP**
>
> *A request for proposal (RFP) is a document that details all required system functionality for a potential purchase. The document is sent to various vendors, who then respond to whether or not and to what degree they can meet the requirements outlined in the document.*

1. vendors
2. contracts
3. bids
4. services

B. Cost-Benefit Analysis

> **Cost-Benefit Analysis**
>
> *This is done to measure the benefits of a new system to its costs. The purpose is to determine whether the potential system will decrease or increase benefits and whether or not it decreases or increases cost for the organization. The analysis is very helpful in justifying the selection of one system over another.*

1. dollar values assigned to the cost and benefit of a proposed system
2. dollar values are compared
3. techniques used to accomplish cost-benefit analysis
   a. break-even point: point at which net revenues equals costs exactly; at this point there is no loss or profit
      i. break-even point is the point at which the net revenue line crosses the total cost line or the point at which the old system costs equal the new system costs
      ii. after the break-even point, the system should begin to generate moneys as compared to old system

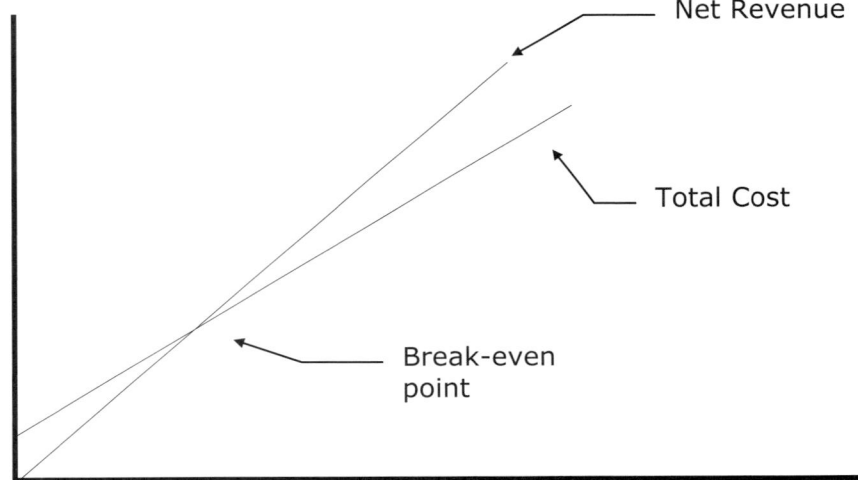

   b. payback period
   c. return on investment
   d. internal rate of return

C. Product-Line Management

VII. Controls of the Department's Financial Condition
   A. Variance reports
   B. Productivity reports
   C. Statistical reports
   D. Budget reports
   E. Payroll reports

VIII. Reimbursement
   A. Chargemaster
      1. database of goods and services
      2. charges associated with CPT/HCPCS codes
      3. elements include
         a. charge code
         b. item description
         c. general ledger key
         d. revenue code
         e. insurance code mapping
         f. charge
         g. activity date status
   B. Claims processing
      1. accumulating charges for services
      2. submitting claims for reimbursement
      3. ensuring claims are satisfied
   C. Accounts receivable
      1. a current asset
      2. charges to be paid for services rendered
      3. analysis of accounts receivable
         a. accounts receivable report

References for Financial Management

Administrative Office Management 12th Edition
   Odgers, Pattie and Kelling, B. Lewis
   Published by: Thompson Learning (South-Western Educational Publishing)

The Effective Health Care Supervisor, 4th Edition
   McConnell, Charles R
   Published by: Jones & Bartlett (previously by Aspen)

Health Information: Management of a Strategic Resource, 2nd Edition
   Abdelhak, Mervat; Grostick, Sara; Hanken, Mary Alice; Jacobs, Ellen; editors
   Published by: W. B. Saunders (Harcourt Health Sciences Company)

Health Information Management: Concepts, Principles, and Practice
   LaTour, Kathleen L. and Eichenwald, Shirley; editors
   Published by: the American Health Information Management Association (AHIMA)

Health Information Management Technology: An Applied Approach
   Johns, Merida L., Editor
   Published by: the American Health Information Management Association (AHIMA)

Introduction to Health Information Technology
   Davis, Nadina and Lacour, Melissa
   Published by W. B. Saunders (Harcourt Health Sciences Company) 2002

Management Principles for Health Professions 2nd Edition
   Liebler, Joan Gratto; Levine, Ruth Ellen; Rothman, Jeffrey
   Published by: Jones & Bartlett (previously by Aspen)

Management of Health Information Functions and Applications
   Mattingly, Rozella
   Published by: Delmar Learning

Management Skills for the New Health Care Supervisor, 3rd Edition
   Umiker, William
   Published by: Jones & Bartlett (previously by Aspen)

APPENDICES

Tools of the Trade

The following appendices are examples of "tools" that can aid you with your study plans. Some of these tools are meant to help you focus, plan and track your study activities; while others are constructed to assist you in organizing the study information. Be aware that these tools are simply a means to an end. Successfully passing the registration exam is the ultimate end. It is not essential that all of these tools be used. An attempt to incorporate all of these tools may actually hinder, rather than help, your study endeavors. You should choose those tools that are most appropriate for your study environment. They can, and should be, adapted to meet your learning style and study needs. Some of these tools were clarified in other sections of this manual, some are self-explanatory and others include a description as to their suggested use.

These appendices as well as a complete listing of the domains, subdomains and task competencies are provided in MSWord and PDF files on the accompanying CD-ROM.

READING/STUDY JOURNAL

TEXT	PAGE #	IMPORTANT CONCEPTS

IMPORTANT NOTES
Content Area

1 TOPIC

What is the topic? Give a brief description of content to be reviewed.

2 RESOURCE

Name of resource (text, notes, manuals etc.) and page number that the topic can be found.

3 LIST THE IMPORTANT DETAILS

Be sure to emphasize the points that are unfamiliar. Summarize the information and use, if possible, only key words and phrases from the resource. You are more likely to understand and remember the information if you use your own words and not those of the resource.

SAMPLE STUDY SCHEDULE

I. June, July and August

    A. Organize
        1. Domains, Subdomains and Tasks
        2. course syllabi
        3. outlines
        4. notes
        5. textbooks

    B. Construct Journal
        1. identify important/significant points and concepts
        2. identify the location of the information (i.e. notes, textbooks etc.)
        3. examine and review journal weekly
        4. identify your strengths and weaknesses for each content area

    C. Organize a Study Group

    D. Create, Design, Construct Study Tools
        1. to do list
        2. Gantt chart
        3. Time table
        4. other

II. September

    A. Review
        1. revise journal
        2. divide the identified weak areas into segments
        3. construct new time charts or other appropriate tools

III. October (or 1 week before the exam)

    A. Cramming
        1. construct fact sheet
            a. identify the 25 most important points to remember
            b. three (3) days prior to exam, identify the ten (10) most important points to remember
        2. make a test run to examination site
        3. ensure that all necessary materials that can accompany you to exam are ready and available (i.e. coding books, pencils and calculator - with a new battery)

    B. Remind yourself of the story **The Little Engine That Could.**-- "I think I can, I think I can, I think I can". Stay positive.

WEEKLY STUDY-TIME CHART

DAY	MANAGEMENT		LEGAL		CODING	
Sunday						
Monday						
Tuesday						
Wednesday						
Thursday						
Friday						
Saturday						
Sunday						
Monday						
Tuesday						
Wednesday						
Thursday						

STUDY/TIME CHART

TASK / ACTIVITY	WEEK OF					
	1	**2**	**3**	**4**	**5**	**6**

STUDY SCHEDULE

Week of_____

Monday		Tuesday	
Begin at	Plan	Begin at	Plan

Wednesday		Thursday	
Begin at	Plan	Begin at	Plan

GANTT CHART

STUDY SCHEDULE																					
MANAGEMENT	JULY 1							JULY 8							JULY 15						
	S	M	T	W	T	F	S	S	M	T	W	T	F	S	S	M	T	W	T	F	S
Domain V Subdomain A Task 3																					
Domain V Subdomain B Task 4																					
Domain V Subdomain B Task 1																					
Domain V Subdomain A Task 6																					
Domain V Subdomain A Task 12																					

Key

Planned Time\Actual time

I want to complete the following activities:

1.
2.
3.
4.
5.
6.
7.
8.
9.
10.

Note: You can change the calendar dates to reflect your actual month and days.

TO DO LIST (A)

DATE:	
Goals for the week:	

Priority	**TO DO {Study Activities}**
1 2 3 4 5	
1 2 3 4 5	
1 2 3 4 5	
1 2 3 4 5	
1 2 3 4 5	
1 2 3 4 5	
1 2 3 4 5	
1 2 3 4 5	
1 2 3 4 5	
1 2 3 4 5	
1 2 3 4 5	
1 2 3 4 5	
1 2 3 4 5	
1 2 3 4 5	
1 2 3 4 5	
1 2 3 4 5	

TO DO LIST (B)

Things To Do For _____

Topic

- [ ] _____
- [ ] _____
- [ ] _____
- [ ] _____
- [ ] _____
- [ ] _____
- [ ] _____
- [ ] _____
- [ ] _____
- [ ] _____
- [ ] _____

FACT SHEET

	Reference	Content Area
1.		
2.		
3.		
4.		
5.		
6.		
7.		
8.		
9.		
10.		
11.		
12.		
13.		
14.		
15.		
16.		
17.		
18.		
19.		
20.		
21.		
22.		
23.		
24.		
25.		

MAPPING

Mapping is a method of active study that aids in condensing information into segments, making the study process more manageable. Below are a model and an example of this technique. As you begin to study, "map" the information rather than simply reading the information. This will increase your retention and comprehension of the information since it requires that you think in a critical mode.

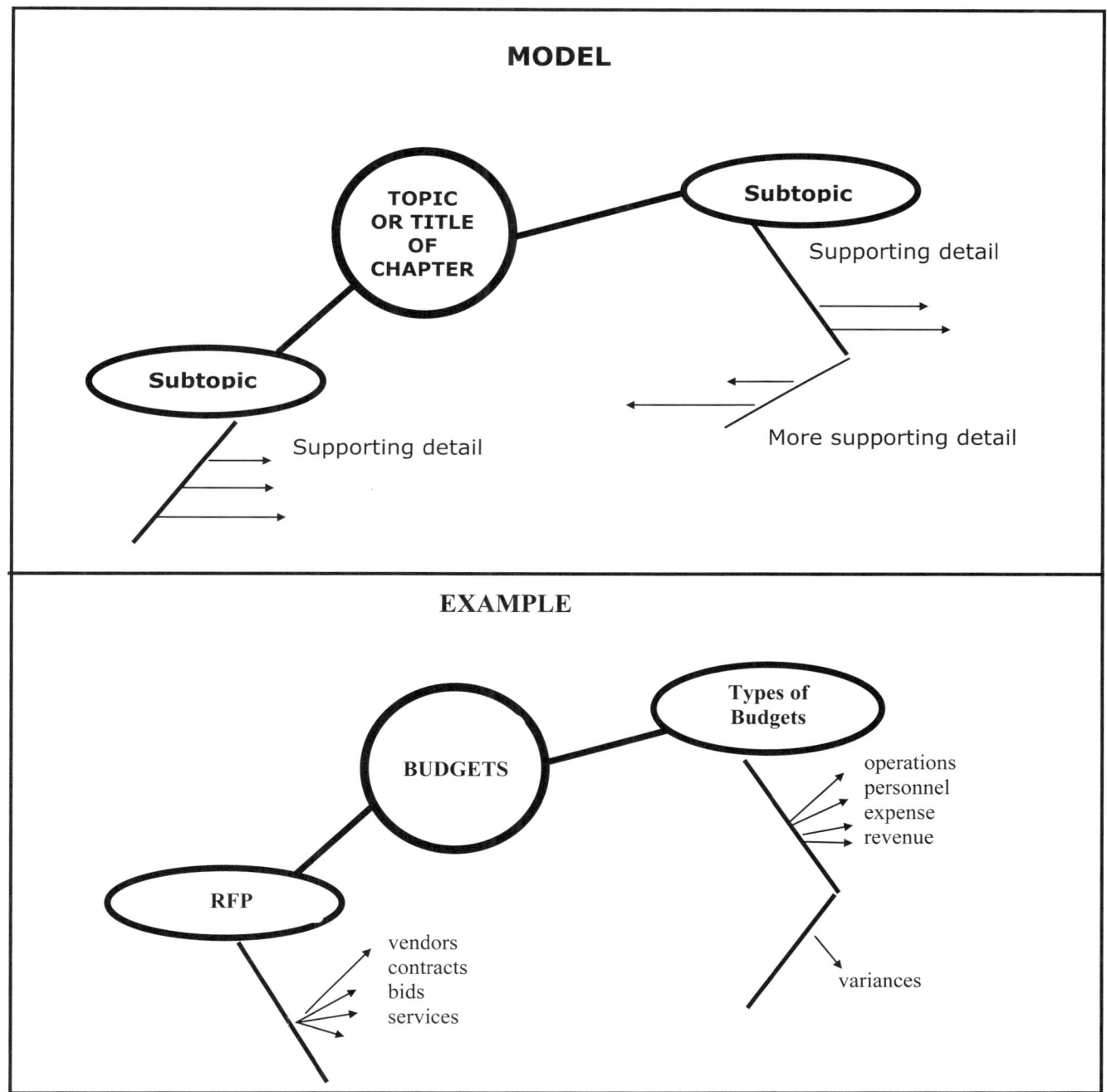

BOOK COVER: Back

These book covers (Appendices IXa and IXb) can be used on any book size or shape. Just cut to fit. The purpose of this study tool is to keep track of particular content, for whatever purpose, from your reference textbooks. A great deal of time is lost trying to recall where certain information can be found. By using this tool, specific information that is desired from textbooks is readily available. The information that has been deemed significant is noted, along with the page number. Fold the paper along the dotted line, the topic and page section should be on the outside of the text and the "This Book Belongs To" section is folded inside the textbook to hold it in place.

THIS BOOK BELONGS TO	TOPIC	PAGE
Juan Doe 5555 N. west Chicago, IL 312-555-1212		

BOOK COVER: Front

TOPIC	PAGE	THIS BOOK BELONGS TO:
		Juan Doe 5555 N. West Chicago, IL 312-555-1212

TEST ANALYSIS WORKSHEET

One of the best ways to prepare for a standardized test is to practice taking tests. Using any test, simulate the test taking environment. Immediately following completion of the test, correct and score the test. Note the test results on a form such as this sample. Analyze the test, making note of your strengths and weakness. Study efforts should now focus on the weaknesses. After a space of time, re-take the same test. Score and analyze. At this time, comparisons can be made between the pre and post- tests. Analyze the results. Are there differences? In what ways? Did the additional study efforts in the areas of weaknesses have any impact on the post-test results? After this analysis, the direction of your study efforts can be re-directed.

PRE-TEST	POST-TEST:
Number Right _____	Number Right _____
Percentage _____	Percentage _____

STRENGTHS/WEAKNESSES	STRENGTHS/WEAKNESSES
1.	1.
2.	2.
3.	3.
4.	4.
5.	5.
6.	6.
7.	7.
8.	8.
9.	9.
10.	10.
11.	11.
12.	12.
13.	13.
14.	14.
15.	15.
16.	16.
17.	17.
18.	18.
19.	19.
20.	20.

STUDY GROUP WORKSHEET

Action Items

Date_____

Topic_____

Leader_____

Action	Person Responsible	Due Date	Status

Notes

STUDY CALENDAR

TASKS	MONTH OF:	
	MONDAY	*THURSDAY*
		1
	5	8
	12	15
	19	22
	26	29
	TUESDAY	*FRIDAY*
		2
	6	9
	13	16
	20	23
	27	30
	WEDNESDAY	*SATURDAY*
		3
	7	10
	14	17
	21	24
	28	31

NOTE: This table is dated based on July 2004 calendar dates. You can modify it to fit your personal schedule.

INDEX

EVALUATION FORM FOR THE BOOK

As we have learned through quality improvement concepts, there is always the opportunity to do something better. Therefore, if you have constructive suggestions for improving the book, please let us know. We invite your input and feedback.

Please rate each of the following aspects of this book on a scale of 1 to 5, where:
5 is excellent, 4 is above average, 3 is average, 2 is below average, and 1 is poor

Depth/completeness of coverage	5	4	3	2	1
Organization of material	5	4	3	2	1
Study tips	5	4	3	2	1
Appropriate level of writing	5	4	3	2	1
Cover design and attractiveness	5	4	3	2	1
Overall design and layout of book	5	4	3	2	1
Overall satisfaction with book	5	4	3	2	1

Would you recommend this book to future graduates studying for the national examinations?

RHIA ☐ Yes ☐ No

RHIT ☐ Yes ☐ No

What can we do to make this book better for you to use?_____
_____
_____
_____

Thank you!

Mail to: **Professional Review Guides, Inc.**
              P. O. Box 528
              St. Petersburg, Florida 33731
Phone: **(727) 526-6-3163**
Toll Free: **(888) 383-PRG1 ~ or ~ 1- (888) 383-7741**
FAX: **(727) 526-4474**
E-mail: **pjsprg@aol.com**
Web site: **www.prgpublishing.com**

EVALUATION FORM FOR THE CD-ROM

As we have learned through quality improvement concepts, there is always the opportunity to do something better. Therefore, if you have constructive suggestions for improving the CD-ROM provided with the book, please let us know. We invite your input and feedback.

Please indicate whether you are   ☐ Student   ☐ Educator

What did you use the CD-ROM for? (Check all that apply)
☐   For personal exam preparation
☐   Other (please elaborate)   _____

_____
_____
_____
_____

Would you recommend the CD-ROM to:

RHIA Exam Candidates	☐ Yes	☐ No
RHIT Exam Candidates	☐ Yes	☐ No
HIM Educators	☐ Yes	☐ No

How can we improve this product for you?_____

_____
_____
_____
_____
_____
_____
_____

Please attach additional comments if you have further suggestions. Thank you!

2004 PRG PUBLISHING
PRODUCT ORDER FORM

Bill To & Ship To:

_____

_____

_____

City _____ State ___ Zip _____

Phone #: (_____) _____

Fax #: (_____) _____

Affiliation: _____

Organization: _____

☐ *Please check box if you would like to be signed up to receive e-mails about our New Releases, Best Sellers, and Special Offers!!!*
    E-Mail Address: _____

TO PLACE AN ORDER OR MAKE A PAYMENT:

Call: (800) 347-7707   **Fax:** (606) 647-5963

Mail: Thomson Delmar Learning
    Attn: Order Fulfillment
    10650 Toebben Drive
    Independence, KY 41051

Or visit our website at
www.delmarhealthcare.com
Questions? Email us at info@delmar.com

PAYMENT METHOD:

___ Purchase Order   ___ Check   ___ Credit Card
Credit Card Type: **(American Express, MasterCard, Visa, Discover)**

Credit Card/PO #: _____

Expiration Date: _____

Signature: _____

Tax Exempt #: _____
*A **detailed invoice** will be included with your order!*

Qty	ISBN	Author – 2004 Titles	Price
_____	1-9321-5214-8	Preparation Guide for the RHIA & RHIT Certification Examinations	$29.95
_____	1-9321-5213-X	Professional Review Guide for the RHIA & RHIT Examinations w/ CD-ROM	$64.95
_____	1-9321-5215-6	Professional Review Guide for the CCS Examination w/ CD-ROM	$64.95
_____	1-9321-5216-4	Professional Review Guide for the CCS-P Examination w/ CD-ROM	$64.95
_____	1-9321-5217-2	Professional Review Guide for the CCA Examination w/ CD-ROM	$64.95
_____	1-9321-5218-0	Professional Review Guide for the CHP, CHS, & CHPS Exams w/ CD-ROM	$89.95
_____	0-9704-5723-5	PRG Quick Notes: A Reference Set for Coding	$21.95
_____	0-9704-5726-X	PRG Quick Notes: CPT Procedural Coding	$6.50
_____	0-9704-5725-1	PRG Quick Notes: for Billing	$6.50
_____	0-9704-5727-8	PRG Quick Notes: Release on Information	$6.50
_____	1-9321-5205-9	PRG Quick Notes: HIPAA Privacy Basics	$6.50
_____	1-9321-5206-7	PRG Quick Notes: Inpatient ICD-9-CM Coding	$6.50
_____	1-9321-5207-5	PRG Quick Notes: Outpatient ICD-9-Coding	$6.50
_____	1-9321-5208-3	PRG Quick Notes: Pharmacology	$6.50
_____	1-9321-5209-1	PRG Quick Notes: Laboratory	$6.50

Total Order: _____
Add State Tax (%): _____
Shipping/Handling: _____
Total Amount Paid: _____

Shipping Options (Please Check One):

☐ UPS Ground: $7.00 First Book, $2.50 each additional
☐ UPS 3rd Day Air: $12.00 First Book, $4.00 each additional
☐ UPS 2nd Day Air: $16.00 First Book, $4.50 each additional

☐ UPS Next Day Air: $25.00 First Book, $8.00 each additional
☐ Foreign Book Rate: $7.00 First Book, $2.50 each additional
☐ Foreign Air Mail: $25.00 First Book, $8.00 each additional